Round Robin Quilts

Friendship Quilts
of the '90s and Beyond

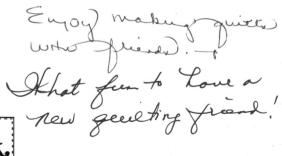

Martha —
Cherish . . . .
Quilts to Share,
Patricia Magaret
Friends who care.
Donna Slusser

Pat Maixner Magaret & Donna Ingram Slusser

Enjoy making quilts
with friends! —
What fun to have a
new quilting friend!

That Patchwork Place ®

Credits

Editor-in-Chief	Barbara Weiland
Technical Editor	Barbara Weiland
Managing Editor	Greg Sharp
Copy Editor	Liz McGehee
Proofreaders	Tina Cook
	Kathleen Timko
Design Director	Judy Petry
Text and Cover Designer	Cheryl Senecal
Typesetter	Cheryl Senecal
Photographer	Brent Kane
Illustrator	Laurel Strand

Round Robin Quilts: Friendship Quilts of the '90s and Beyond ©
© 1994 by Pat Maixner Magaret and Donna Ingram Slusser

That Patchwork Place, Inc.,
PO Box 118, Bothell, WA 98041-0118 USA

Printed in Hong Kong
99 98 97 96   6 5 4 3

Library of Congress Cataloging-in-Publication Data
Magaret, Pat Maixner
    Round Robin quilts : friendship quilts of the 90's and beyond / Pat Maixner Magaret and Donna Ingram Slusser.
        p. cm.
    Includes bibliographical references.
    ISBN 1-56477-065-6:
    1. Patchwork—Patterns. 2. Quilting—Patterns. 3. Friendship quilts. I. Slusser, Donna Ingram. II. Title.
TT835.M2713 1994
746.46—dc20   94-21147
                                                            CIP

Dedication

To the quilt groups we belong to: Patchin' People, Palouse Patchers, Washington State Quilters (Spokane Chapter) and especially Stitch 'n Study. All the members are as different as the patches in a quilt, yet we are stitched together with friendship and bound together with love.

Acknowledgments

With thanks and appreciation to:
    Our husbands, Lloyd and David. Our children, Alan, Kirstin, and Larry; and Craig, Nathan, and Anna. While they will always be "our kids," they've grown up to be our friends.
    The owners and their friends of the treasured quilts that are pictured in this book: Thine Bloxham, Pam Bryceson, Kathleen Butts, Eleanor Cole, Diane Coombs, Christine Davis, Joan Dawson, Lorna Druffel, Marta Estes, Rosy Ferner, Lori Fleisher, Michelle Goodson, Gayle Hazen, Kerry Hoffman, Judy Hopkins, Terry Johnson-Huhta, Ute Jarasitis, Susan Jones, Janine Lauderback, Kathy Marks, Nancy J. Martin, Judy Murrah, Rachel Nichols, Gayle Noyes, Ardell Parkin, Janie Perino, Shirley Perryman, Juliann Phillips, Lee Philpott, Barbie Pratt, Sara Quattlebaum, Ursula Reikes, Laura Reinstatler, Jeanie Renfro, Rock Creek Quilters, Christine Schultz, Marion Shelton, Barbara Stellmon, Nadene Stephenson, Cynthia Stroo, Corlis Taylor, Jean VanBockel, Barbara Weiland, Kathy White, Dotti Wilke, Sharon Wiser.
    The husbands of our Stitch 'n Study friends, who pick up the slack when deadlines are near, who eat oatmeal for dinner, who vacuum when snippets of threads hide the color of the carpet, and who have to sleep with the cat or dog until the quilter comes to bed.
    Judy Hopkins, who, in her book, One-of-a-Kind Quilts, pioneered the concept of using small blocks around a larger theme block and placing them on a 4" x 4" gridded vertical design wall.
    The Department of Parks and Recreation, City of Pullman, Washington, for use of the photograph of the Wonders of Washington quilt.
    The Nebraska State Historical Society, for use of the photograph of the Crazy Quilt.
    Arline J. Yarbrough and Gregg Rothenberger for sharing their family treasures.
    The entire staff of That Patchwork Place for their generous help, which is always extended with gracious friendliness.
    Each other, for being not only co-authors and co-teachers, but first and always, friends.
    Abby, Lily, and Muffin, for their unflagging friendship.

Table of Contents

Introduction

Because of the written words and needlework skills of our ancestors, we can travel through time and share their good times and bad, plenty and want, joy and sadness. Through it all, we feel a kinship and a sense of heritage because we have quilting, too.

Leslie Lewis

Throughout our nation's history, quilts and friends have shared something very basic—both have warmed our souls. Whether in a crude cabin on the pioneer prairie of long ago or in an upscale condo in a modern city, quilts and good friends go together like cake and ice cream. They tell the stories of the lives and the times of their makers. In the past, quilts served as one of the only outlets for female creative expression.

The American quilt was born out of necessity to provide warm bedcovers and hangings for doors and windows. The early colonists and pioneers endured many hardships and sometimes they had to call upon all of their skills to survive. Even in the toughest of times, the need for friendship and fellowship brought women together. As early as the mid-1700s, American women were meeting to socialize and work together on their needlework projects, including quiltmaking.

In the 1800s, as Americans began moving west, their rural lifestyle meant there were often long distances between farms and homes. The wife or young mother was sometimes the loneliest person on the western frontier. Hard work and the demands of daily life left little or no time for social activities. Even though they lived under primitive conditions, helping to clear the land and grow simple crops, pioneer women made time to express their creative longings in needlework and quilts. They hoarded fabric scraps, sometimes for years. The visiting peddler making his annual rounds was often their only contact; they came to rely on him for information about new fabrics and quilt patterns. Even then, precious money saved for a beautiful piece of fabric might instead be spent on a new utensil or other necessities, such as shoes.

Whenever these women could snatch a spare moment from their daily duties, they gathered their fabric scraps, cut them into patches, and sewed them together to create quilts. They looked forward to meeting new neighbors with whom they could share ideas, recipes, laughter, and tears. They looked forward to get-togethers to do communal work—such as quilting. Needlework skills drew them together, and total strangers found they had a common bond.

In the 1830s, a new product took quiltmaking in a new direction. Until that time, ink was usually homemade and unreliable. Many recipes for ink contained iron and tannin, which, when used on cloth, caused the fibers to deteriorate over time. The new ink did not contain iron and therefore did not ultimately damage the cloth. At the same time, "annuals" or "albums" became popular New Year's gifts. These were blank books in which the recipient could record the year's events. Women filled the pages with poetry, quotations, and art work, often asking visitors and friends to make additions. *Godey's Lady's Book and Magazine* was a popular publication of the day and a source of inspiration for women of the nineteenth century. It contained quotations and poetry that they often added to their annuals and albums and to new types of quilts—Friendship and Album quilts.

Crazy Quilt by members of the Ladies Aid Society of the Methodist Episcopal Church, 1893, Filley, Nebraska, 69" x 86". The Ladies Aid Society made the blocks that contain their names. They raised money by charging individuals ten cents each to have their names placed on the quilt back. The member who collected the most names and dimes won and finished the quilt. Courtesy of the Nebraska State Historical Society.

Signature Quilt, 1917, Pennsylvania, 70" x 81". Signatures of friends and family members were embroidered on this quilt. Courtesy of Kathleen H. Butts.

Album quilts were popular in the 1840s and 1850s. As the name implies, they were made like album pages on cloth. They remind us of scrapbooks and albums, where every page is different. Needlework and appliqué replaced artwork; poetry and prose were penned in ink on the quilt blocks. As many as thirty or forty people made blocks for one quilt. Because the quiltmakers were often very competitive, many of the finished quilts were quite elaborate. They were usually made to commemorate a specific event—an expression of thanks for a job well done, good luck to newlyweds, or farewell to those moving on. No two blocks were identical—all were made and signed by a different friend or individual.

Some of the most beautiful Album quilts are the Baltimore Album quilts produced between 1846 and 1852. They are characterized by their elaborate, one-of-a-kind designs, beautiful fabrics, extensive use of appliqué, and excellent workmanship. Baskets, wreaths, bouquets of flowers, pictorial scenes, and fraternal symbols are hallmarks of these special quilts.

A variation of the Album quilt was the Freedom quilt, popular until the early nineteenth century. At that time, a young man often served as an apprentice or was legally bound to his parents or guardians, who received his earnings. When the young man reached legal age, 21, his mother held a party and invited his friends. Each guest was expected to bring a quilt block to share. These usually depicted patriotic symbols or masculine subjects. The blocks were then assembled and quilted under his mother's direction—possibly the last time "Mother" could have her say. The finished quilt was presented to the young man as a symbol of his independence.

Album quilts had their origins in Pennsylvania and Maryland, but the idea spread to other parts of the country as many Americans joined the great western migration. As families moved, women shared their ideas and patterns, and soon women in other parts of the country developed their own interpretations of this style of quiltmaking.

Soon Album quilts gave way to less elaborate Friendship quilts. When good friends left the area, the ones left behind needed a tangible way of saying "farewell," and the Friendship quilt was born. This type of quilt usually consisted of a single block pattern (pieced or appliquéd). The Chimney Sweep and Album Patch blocks were popular patterns used for these quilts.

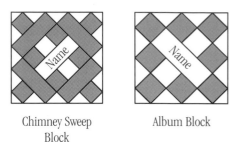

Chimney Sweep
Block

Album Block

One maker would make the blocks, reserving the same area in each block for signatures, dates, quotes, Biblical verses, and artwork, and hand them out to friends to personalize and then return for assembly. A group of friends completed the gift with hand quilting. This type of quilt is still being made today as a token of friendship.

Often, a Friendship medley quilt was made during the farewell party. People brought their fabrics and quilt patterns to the party and used their creativity and skills to make a block. After all the blocks were signed, they were sewn together and quilted or tied.

Sometimes a woman collected fabrics from each of her friends as a special kind of remembrance, then used each one to make a special block. Usually all the blocks were of the same design. If there was time to finish the blocks before she left to go west, she had her friends sign their blocks. Just imagine the quiltmaker, far away from home and familiar faces, remembering her friends and loved ones with fondness as she looked at the individual blocks in her quilt.

Album and Friendship quilts had a very special meaning to their recipients. Emotions were woven between each thread. Often the quilts were respected, treasured, and used only for special occasions. Because of this, many old Album and Friendship quilts are in excellent condition, even today, and on display in museums.

The popularity of group-made quilts declined after the Civil War due to low morale and interest in the Victorian Crazy quilt that emerged in the 1870s. During the Victorian era, the Autograph or Signature quilt was also popular. The quiltmaker collected signatures of friends and family—even autographs of famous people—and then embroidered or inked them in a random fashion on the quilt top. Sometimes, the names would be arranged so they formed a circle or other design.

The Quotation quilt was a popular variation of the Autograph quilt during the 1880s. Some of these quilts are still being made today. Friends are invited to either make a block and include a quotation on it, or the owner makes blocks and passes them out to her friends to sign and add a saying or short poem. Scripture quotations were commonly added to early Quotation quilts.

Another type of Signature quilt was the Opportunity quilt or "fund-raiser". Women joined together in friendship to make quilts in support of their favorite crusade, whether it was the Women's Christian Temperance Union or the local church and its missionary work. Quilts had open areas for many signatures, and anyone signing the quilt made a donation. These quilts are the forerunners of the Opportunity quilts made today to support charities and various causes.

Since the Bicentennial in 1976, quiltmaking and, more specifically, group quiltmaking, has made a comeback and is no longer considered "woman's work." Men and children are joining in and contributing their efforts and skills. The bond of sisterhood is now including brothers as well.

Today's technology shortens communication time and eliminates geographical distance. Computer networks enhance information sharing and friendships "across the miles."

Friendship quilts are for everyone. As in the past, they are still being made for those special friends who are moving away and to commemorate other events, such as having a baby or relinquishing the presidency of a quilt guild.

Love from One Friend to Another by Nadene Stephenson, 1989, Edmonds, Washington, 26¼" x 34½". Ladies of the Block quilt group members Beverly Payne, Carol Porter, Nancy Sweeney, Eileen Westfall, Leanne Ober, Carol Hart, Marion Shelton, Marta Estes, Teresa Haskins, Ferol Yust, and Sue von Jentzen used their own fabrics to make House blocks for Nadene. This charming wall hanging expresses love from their homes to hers.

On the grass-roots level, school children are making Friendship quilts in the classroom. The Soviet-American Peace Quilt is an example of an international Friendship quilt, made through the combined efforts of quiltmakers from different countries to promote peace.

Most important of all, Friendship quilts are being made for friends, by friends.

In the late 1980s, a new type of Friendship quilt began to emerge. Instead of exchanging blocks or collecting fabrics and signatures, friends passed their projects among group members, who each made an addition to every quilt top. They became known as Round Robin quilts.

Donna's acquaintance with the Round Robin concept started in early childhood. Her mother and several college friends decided to stay in touch with each other after graduation. They circulated letters from each other in one big envelope, which would make its rounds among the participants several times each year. Donna remembers her mother's excitement when she opened the mailbox and found the bulky envelope waiting. It would take an afternoon with several cups of tea to catch up on the latest events of her friends' lives, the newest babies, and eventually, the children's weddings. Then it was her turn to remove her old letter and write a new one to slip into the envelope before sending it on its way.

The Round Robin Friendship quilts being made today reflect this letter-writing tradition. There are many possible variations, but essentially, a Round Robin quilt begins with a group of friends deciding they want to work on projects for each other. After a meeting to write the rules and guidelines for the project, each group member makes a block (or other specified piece), following the guidelines for the project. The piece is then placed in a box with other items specified in the guidelines and passed to someone else in the group, who adds to the project. This continues until each person has taken a turn to add their work to each growing quilt top. Each addition contributes to the total design of the project. Wall hangings, bed quilts, and even vests and jackets lend themselves to the Round Robin idea.

We belong to a group that exchanges birthday blocks throughout the year. In the spring of 1991, the group decided to work on special

Signature Quilt (Wagon Wheels and Leaves), 1899, 70" x 63". This signature quilt includes embroidered dates from October 1898 through January 1899. Courtesy of Arline J. Yarbrough.

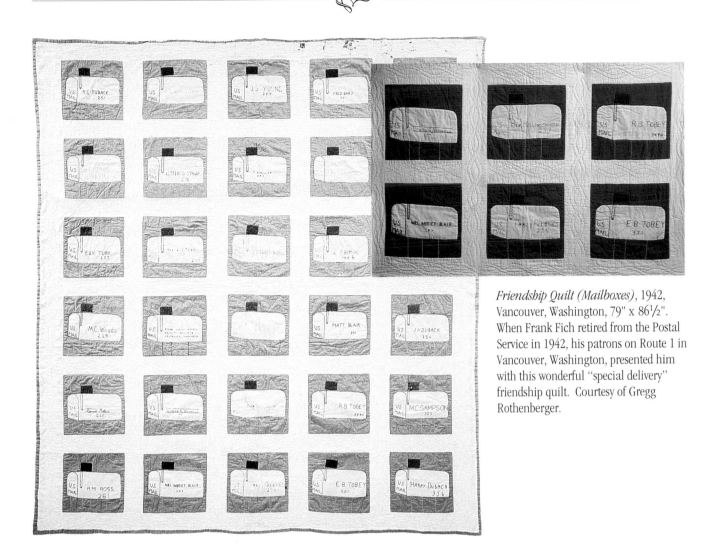

Friendship Quilt (Mailboxes), 1942, Vancouver, Washington, 79" x 86½". When Frank Fich retired from the Postal Service in 1942, his patrons on Route 1 in Vancouver, Washington, presented him with this wonderful "special delivery" friendship quilt. Courtesy of Gregg Rothenberger.

pass-around projects instead of making individual blocks for each other. Each person cut out a background piece and appliquéd a few motifs on it to set the theme, colors, and mood for the completed project. These backgrounds were passed among the group, round-robin style, with each member adding motifs that carried out the theme. With a few modifications, this became the Add-On Appliqué Round Robin project featured in this book, beginning on page 56.

We also belong to several quilt guilds, including the Palouse Patchers in Moscow, Idaho. Guild members started a Merry-Go-Round Medallion project in the fall of 1991, with each participant making the center block for a medallion-style quilt to get the project started. As borders were added, the excitement grew. These projects made a wonderful display when the quilt tops were hung and exhibited at the May 1992 guild meeting.

In the spring of 1993, we had a brainstorm for a new type of pass-around project. The idea was to place a large theme block on a piece of gridded polyester fleece and pass it among friends so they could each add small blocks to the project. The Around-the-Block quilt was born and is featured in this book, beginning on page 64.

One of the best parts about writing this book has been seeing these new types of Friendship quilts. They are truly beautiful and have something special about them that the viewer not only sees but senses with the heart. The owners and makers of these quilts wrote wonderful comments on the information forms they returned to us with snapshots of their quilts. These words are too precious to leave in a file, tucked away in a drawer, so we have incorporated them into the text. Enjoy the thoughts of these quiltmakers as they share ideas about quilting and friendship with all of us.

What's Ahead

We designed this book as a manual to help you organize a successful Round Robin project. It contains helpful information for anyone participating in such a process and includes photographs of completed Round Robin quilts that will amaze, inspire, and delight you! This book is also a tribute to friendship.

Getting Started

The chapter on getting started spells out fundamental ideas as well as details to help your project begin successfully. There are suggested tasks for a coordinating committee and hints for conducting meetings so that everyone has an opportunity to contribute before the group reaches consensus on major issues. Basic guidelines for all types of groups are presented. Optional guidelines are given for groups that want more structure. Pick and choose so that the structure of the project meets the needs of your group. You'll find ideas for the "unveiling" of the finished projects when they are returned to the owners, including suggestions for a reunion party to commemorate the completion of the quilted projects.

Quotations from quiltmakers whose projects are pictured in this book are woven into the text throughout the book. Their thoughtful, insightful, and occasionally humorous comments shed insight on the process and will help you complete your project successfully and have fun, too.

Border Beauties

The chapter on the Border Beauties type of Round Robin quilt is encouragement for those who have always wanted to make a medallion-style quilt. This project begins with the owner making a center block and each participant adding a border until the quilt top is complete.

In this chapter you will find information on how to make a successful medallion quilt, including planning a theme block and borders. You will find it helpful, even if you want to make the entire quilt top by yourself.

A section on border engineering takes the fear out of the mathematics required to make borders fit. Another section on fudging helps correct the sizing problems you might encounter along the way. We have included patterns for several center blocks as well as ideas for borders.

Add-On Appliqué

The Add-On Appliqué Round Robin quilt gives quilters a chance to practice their appliqué techniques. The owner/initiator creates a large background piece and appliqués a few motifs on it to set the theme or create the mood for the project. The backgrounds are then passed around the group and participants add motifs that carry out the ideas of the theme. Theme ideas and information about backgrounds are included.

Around-the-Block

For the Around-the-Block Round Robin quilt project, the owner/initiator makes a theme block, and participants make smaller blocks that coordinate with the theme. Ideas for theme blocks and descriptions of supporting blocks are included in this chapter. A chart with suggestions for specific block layouts helps in the planning process. A second chart shows simple connector blocks that can be added.

Round Robin Variations

Ideas for other types of Round Robin projects, including garments, are featured in the chapter "Round Robin Variations."

Design Basics

This section is particularly helpful if you are making Add-On-Appliqué or Around-the-Block projects. The brief discussion about basic elements and principles of design guides you toward making a unified composition.

Finishing Up & Quiltmaking Basics

Once your quilt has completed its journey, you'll find tips on how to complete the design. Border selection, backing options, quilting suggestions, signing, and labels are discussed in detail. Everything you need to know about how to finish your project is included in the section on "Quiltmaking Basics." It is a compact and concise guide to help you with all your quiltmaking projects.

We hope you and your friends meet the challenge and try the friendship projects in this book. Join us as we explore the possibilities of making Round Robin quilts, Friendship quilts of the '90s and beyond!

Getting Started

True friendship is not "a fad,"
Is not "in season."
It lasts forever
Without a reason.
  Evelyn Axtell Barrows

  Successful Round Robin projects are special. They have a feeling of caring and sharing.

"I really treasure this quilt and appreciate all the thought and work that went into each stitch."
  Nancy J. Martin

  These projects push the limitations we sometimes knowingly and unknowingly impose upon our creativity. We seem to need challenges to stretch ourselves.

"I overcame fear of failure as I accepted challenges in design, color, and techniques. I had to work with colors and color combinations I didn't necessarily like. I had never before created original designs to coordinate with an existing motif. For a beginning quilter like me, it was an excellent stimulus to growth."
  Chris Schultz

"I found myself working with unusual color combinations. I found myself wanting to design something that would integrate with the quilt to make it look like it was made by one person. I realized that if I could push myself and be creative in the context of a group, I could also do it on my own."
  Dotti Wilke

"I had little experience with design work—I described the project as 'designing by the seat of my pants.' It's true—with practice comes confidence."
  Janine Lauderback

"We used to make quilt blocks for each other and exchange them at our monthly meetings. This has been much more exciting, creatively satisfying, and has allowed each of us to express ourselves in a way that those quilt blocks never could!"
  Barbie Pratt

"Creating the Round Robin quilts was one of the most 'stretching,' exciting, and scary things I've ever done. I couldn't wait to start the next one."
  Rachel Nichols

  Creativity takes time.

Joan Hanson wrote in Nancy Martin's journal that accompanied her quilt on the rounds:
"I've finally developed a system for these Round Robin projects.
1. Hang it on the wall and 'live' with it.
2. Cruise every fabric shop within 20 miles and buy lots of fabric.
3. Whine about the project to at least two other members of the group.
4. Design SOMETHING!
5. Borrow more fabric from a friend's vast stash.
6. Sew like a mad woman.
7. Put away all the fabric I bought in step 2 that I didn't use."

  Did we remember to tell you that keeping your sense of humor helps when working on these projects?

Keys to a Successful Round Robin Project

Round Robin projects can be wonderful or they can be disastrous. We have discovered there are three ingredients fundamental to a project's success: enthusiasm, flexibility, and commitment.

Enthusiasm

There is usually a great deal of excitement and enthusiasm at the announcement of a Round Robin project, but occasionally the idea will not take off. Some individuals may not be able to participate for a variety of reasons. Remember, this type of project is not for everyone. Once a group decides to do a Round Robin project, there is usually a lot of excitement, especially when it is time to rotate the projects.

If some of the participants are starting to lose their enthusiasm and are becoming discouraged, have a "checking out" process to see if they can be helped in any way.

Flexibility

Be willing to let go of the control of your project. Be willing to be surprised.

If you get to see your project as it progresses, when one addition doesn't live up to your expectations, wait until the next time or two to see what happens. Quilters are good problem solvers and you will be surprised at some of the unique solutions found to seemingly impossible situations.

This type of project is built around various personalities. Remember that participants do not always work at the same speed, and you might have to adjust deadlines for the completion of a round or two. Be flexible.

Commitment

To be successful, group members must be dedicated and committed to the project. Learning new skills, doing one's best work, and treating everyone's project as if it were your own is important. Remember the Golden Rule of Round Robin quiltmaking: Work on another person's project as you want them to work on yours.

There is also a commitment to keeping to the group's schedule. Those who are "last-minute Annies" will find it helpful to set a personal

"The entire project between our group of friends was such a wonderful experience. Each month when we met to unveil and pass the quilts, it was like a mini-Christmas."
Christine Davis

"The project was an exercise in trust. We had to release control of how our quilts would evolve. It was a challenge to make the monthly additions without using a technique or requirement from another month. We were all surprised at how different the quilts were. We all followed the same guidelines but had such different results."
Juliann Phillips

"Though I had an idea of how I wanted my project to turn out, other people did things I would never have thought to do. It makes the quilt that much more special. It's not exactly what I had in mind— it's better!"
Shirley Perryman

"Make up your mind to appreciate all creative efforts and love your quilt no matter what. Don't have a set idea about what it should look like!"
Thine Bloxham

"Working on another's project presents a special set of problems and challenges. Although I might not have had the same inspiration or enthusiasm for every quilt, I felt the challenge to do good work and to enhance the piece before I sent it on to the next quilter."
Judy Hopkins

The Golden Rule
of Round Robin Quilts

Work on another person's project as you want them to work on yours!

deadline several days before the real one. It is important to allow extra time for interruptions (taking time to cook meals for a hungry family), emergencies (a trip to the fabric shop to find more of that special fabric), and disasters like "I can't believe I snipped off that point!"

If you and a group of your quilting friends are excited about doing a Round Robin project, then let's get started!

The First Gathering (Filing a Flight Plan)

Once the idea for a group project has been proposed, several friends can get together and create a "flight plan." The preliminary meeting is a time for a coordinating committee to do some initial planning. Keep the numbers down so there are not too many diverging ideas. Three is a good number of people for this committee so there is always a tie-breaker when needed.

The first step for the committee is to elect or appoint a spokesperson who will be the "Voice" for this project. This quilter is the main facilitator and should be respected by all the participants. Choose someone who is encouraging, diplomatic, and has a sense of humor!

Also choose a secretary to keep a record of all ideas, decisions, lists of participants, addresses, and phone numbers. Copy and distribute these to all group members.

Appoint an education director or resource person who is responsible for suggesting resources during the project and who will organize workshops or technique classes when they are needed. Select someone who has good technique skills and has access to quilting resources, such as various quilting books and magazines.

Review the guidelines used by other groups to get ideas for your project. These are included under "Sample Group Guidelines" in each of the three different chapters on Round Robin projects. When discussing the guidelines, don't let one person make all the decisions. Come up with several options and let all the participants take part in the first full group meeting so they feel that they, too, have a voice in this process. Allow time for plenty of discussion at the beginning. Use the comments and questions in this chapter to help the group arrive at a consensus about the guidelines to use.

Guidelines for All Groups

In order to establish the guidelines for your group, you will need to make final decisions about the following topics.

Type of Project

Discuss the type of Round Robin project you want to tackle. Which project sounds exciting? Which idea will fly the best (is best-suited to the desires, temperament, and skills of the group members)? Does this project have a purpose other than pure friendship? Will the projects be entered as a group in a quilt show?

This book has plans and ideas for three basic types of Round Robin projects. Border Beauties are medallion-style quilts with pieced borders and one or two optional appliqué borders (pages 20–55). The Add-On Appliqué project is appliqué only (pages 56–63). Around-the-Block projects have a combination of piecing and appliqué techniques (pages 64–78).

Time Schedule

Set tentative guidelines for the beginning and completion dates. How often do you want to rotate the projects—monthly, bimonthly, quarterly? Be flexible when considering prospective participants for your group.

> "There seemed to be a process repeated each time I received a project. Some internal time clock that started with evaluation, concept organization, and then execution. It just couldn't be hurried."
> Gayle Noyes

> "When projects are not passed along on time, it makes less time for the next person to work on the project."
> Barbara Stellmon

> "Select a group whose members have similar time available for the project. Then double the time you think it will take!"
> Thine Bloxham

Skill Levels

Weigh the issue of similar skill levels. What are the skill levels within the group? Will they be learning new techniques? What about workmanship? Everyone will be more pleased with their completed project if they are not having to make do with less, as far as workmanship is concerned.

Participants in these projects range from relatively new quilters who are just learning to fly to those who are experienced enough to "know all the flock migration patterns." This is probably not a project for true beginners, but for quilters who know what they can accomplish when they set their minds to it. If your group has participants with different levels of experience, hold mini-workshops that focus on techniques required for the project. These learning experiences help alleviate the stress that comes from wondering whether you are doing everything "right."

Another suggestion is to use a "mentor" program in which an experienced quilter is available to answer questions and give advice to a quilter who needs help. Sometimes asking questions is easier when it is on a one-on-one basis.

If a guild is undertaking this project, you will need to break down into small groups. In this case, it might be advisable to place quilters with similar skills together. If workshops or technique classes are planned, they can then be geared to a specific skill level.

✑ Note

If education is offered, do not make it mandatory. Quilters need to be given credit for handling situations and problems on their own.

Group Size

Discuss the prospective participants. It helps if you are all friends. The number of participants depends upon the type of project that is being undertaken. The Border Beauties project works well with four to eight friends. (Remember, the more people who participate in this project, the longer it takes to complete the total rotation process—and the larger the quilt tops become!) The Add-On Appliqué can accommodate any number of quilters and the Around-the-Block works well with five to twelve participants. You can adjust the rules and guidelines to produce a quilt of a particular size.

Rotation

List the names of the participants in the desired rotation order. Each person passes the project on to the person following their name on the list, and the one at the bottom of the list passes to the person at the top. Some groups list the names alphabetically, others draw names out of a hat, some use the order of birthdays, and others arrange people by geographical proximity.

Show-and-Tell: To Keep a Secret or Not

Will there be show-and-tell at each rotation? Some groups prefer to rotate their projects in secrecy so the finished project is a total surprise to the owner when it is unveiled. To keep the secret, the owner leaves the room while their project is "out of the bag."

Other groups prefer to share every project with all members after each rotation. In each of these two scenarios, group members use the show-and-tell time to discuss problems and share ideas. Some group members enjoy this type of guidance and consider it a challenge to integrate the owner's ideas with their own.

Some don't have show-and-tell at all at the rotation meeting, preferring to keep the progression of every project secret until the end. This option works best for experienced quilters who can work on their own and enjoy keeping a secret.

"The quilt was kept a secret from the person who had made the center block. At our meetings, we sent that person out of the room when we showed our progress on the borders. We usually said misleading comments in loud voices so no one would suspect the actual progress of their quilt!"
Kathy White

"Not being able to see our quilts, but hearing the ohs and ahs—pure torture! It was a fun time and eagerly anticipated."

Kathy Marks

"It's amazing how a group of individuals could create such a beautiful quilt without consulting each other. I thank each of them for their creativity."

Barbara Stellmon

For those groups that choose to share their work after each rotation, every exchange time is special. Believe us, no one wants to miss these meetings! It draws the members of the group closer together in friendship. There is also a sharing of ideas among participants. It alleviates some of the fear and anxiety that quilters experience when they feel "under the gun" to create something special on someone else's quilt in a short period of time. Not everyone is a free spirit. Encouragement and sharing create a climate of confidence and creativity.

Another advantage to using these options is that participants can be thinking ahead and planning potential additions to other members' projects, but don't be disappointed if someone uses your idea before the project gets to you. Always keep an open mind!

Final Rotation

The meeting where the projects are returned to the owner/initiators is the time for the final show-and-tell. Plan an exhibit if facilities permit. Bring cameras and plenty of film to this meeting. If a video camera is available, use it to capture owner's reactions when they receive their quilts or other projects. The tape can be played at a later meeting for a trip down memory lane.

Reunion Party

When do you want the quilts to be completely quilted and finished? Plan a tentative date now for this special time of show-and-tell and consider extending the Round Robin idea by planning a progressive dinner for participants and their spouses or special guests. A salad bar luncheon or potluck dinner also makes a festive occasion. Bring cameras and plenty of film to record individuals with their completed quilts or other projects. Don't forget to take a group shot.

Optional Guidelines
Rules or No Rules

Some groups have no rules except the basics, while others like more guidelines. We found that when quilters talk about their Round Robin projects, they feel strongly about whether to have the "rules" or "no rules" format. They usually like the method they used and think it is the best! With the rules format, each round must meet certain specifications, for example, adding a pieced border or placing the center square on point in a Border Beauty project.

Each group needs to make decisions for their project based on information from the members. Be sure the rules are set prior to the beginning of the rotations and are very clear to all members. This helps avoid misunderstandings.

Size of Project

Does the group want a guideline about the finished size of the quilt? If so, determine an approximate finished quilt size. Do you want miniatures, wall quilts, bed quilts, or do you even care? See individual projects for comments and suggestions. Most of the suggested projects are wall-quilt size when returned to their owners.

Owner's Options

Discuss the members' expectations of what will happen to the quilt top after it returns to its originator. Besides adding borders, how much work can the owner do to the project? Do you want to impose a rule that prevents the owner from adding to the project once it is returned? Does the owner have the option to enlarge the project, even to bed-size? In the case of Add-On Appliqué and Around-the-Block projects, the owner may need to add motifs and units to make the project look complete and balanced. Can owners change or move the motifs and units around to their satisfaction? What about overlapping objects?

This issue can be very touchy. There is the "Camp of Purists" who feel Friendship quilts should be just that—Friendship quilts—no alterations or additions allowed! Then there is the "Camp of the Perfectionists," who probably will not finish their quilts unless the design and color are well balanced with all motifs in place and workmanship that is consistent.

Make sure this issue is settled before beginning the project to avoid any misunderstandings.

Items to Include in the Owner's Box

Do you want to ask the owner to include anything in the box with the project? Consider the following:

Fabric

Does each participant include fabric with their project? If so, how many fabrics and how much? Again, some groups prefer to stretch their creativity and not have any fabric guidelines from the owner, other than the colors and fabrics used in the beginning of the project. If the owner includes fabrics to use, the project will have a more coordinated look to it.

Do participants use only the owner's fabrics or can they incorporate some fabrics from their

"No rules are great for stretching creativity. For me, rules would make it more difficult."
Susan Jones

"We had great fun with these quilts because we let the quilt tell us what it needed. Our rules were— no rules!"
Marion Shelton

"Sometimes the rules got in the way of a little more creativity."
Lori Fleisher

"I liked the fact that we were all working on the same type of border at the same time. It gave us a feeling of camaraderie. We could share information about techniques."
Sara Jane Perino

"The rules for each border provided structure and continuity. It was exciting to see how many different interpretations there were of the same format. What a wonderful variety of ideas!
Terry Johnson-Huhta

own stash? Most groups let participants add fabrics from their own collections.

Do people contribute some of the fabric they used to each project's box as it is passed along?

Journal

Decide if you would like to pass a small journal along with each project. This is a way to add to the memories. It is a special record written by the participants for the owner of the quilt. Some groups make their own journals and include clever drawings and quotations. Information to add includes: name and address; a lively recording of experiences while working on the project; the name and source of the pattern used; historical information and research done for the addition.

Label

Does the owner want to send a label along for everyone to sign when the project is passed around or wait until after the final rotation? Labels are another opportunity to have your friends add something special to your project. For ideas, see the photos on page 99. More information about labels appears on pages 97–100.

Resources and Information

In the Add-On Appliqué and Around-the-Block Round Robin quilt projects, it is helpful for each owner to include information about the theme in the project box. Books, magazine articles, and photographs can all serve as inspiration for motifs and block designs.

Inspirational Goodies

Some owners' boxes contain wonderful inspiration. Thoughtful or humorous books, food treats, and lottery tickets have all found their way into project boxes.

The Interlude

After establishing the suggested guidelines, the coordinating committee invites all interested participants to a general meeting for an enthusiastic, upbeat presentation of the Round Robin concept. Be sure to have a copy of this book available at the meeting as well as any real-life examples you might have. These help encourage participation. Be sure to cover each of the following points.

- Explain the Round Robin concept. Reinforce the idea that all participants will end up with a quilt to keep.
- Present all the issues, ideas, and options to the group and listen for feedback. Remember to let everyone have their say.
- Explain the process for the type of Round Robin project you are proposing.
- Discuss the anticipated size of the quilt.
- Talk about the frequency of the rotation system and the breakdown into smaller groups if necessary.
- Get a consensus of the members' preferences regarding various guidelines and finalize them. Be sure everyone clearly understands the decisions that are made.
- Determine if group members would like to have workshops and classes and whether or not they would like to have a mentor program, with more experienced quilters helping less experienced ones.
- Get a commitment from the prospective quilters who want to participate.
- Set a date for when all participants need to have everything ready to go in their pass-around box.
- Set a tentative date for a reunion party when all quilts will be completed.
- Encourage promptness and stress the importance of keeping deadlines.
- Remind everyone of the Golden Rule for Round Robin Quilts: Work on another person's project as you want them to work on yours. Each person needs to strive to do the best job possible when working on every quilt.

Think in terms of making your addition something that will help unify the project.

Takeoff

Shortly after the organizational meeting, the secretary types a copy of the project guidelines and a list of group members with addresses and telephone numbers, rotation order, and pass-along meeting dates. Copies are then distributed to each participant. The education director plans classes and workshops if they are needed.

Meanwhile, the participants are having fun thinking about design possibilities and choosing color schemes. Those involved in the Border Beauties project are hunting for unused blocks they have lying around to see if one of them can be used for a center block. Or, they are deciding which pattern to use to make a new block. Participants of the Add-On Appliqué and Around-the-Block quilts are busy thinking about themes, waiting for the light bulb to go on over their heads, and bumping into one another in the library and bookstores. As you plan your block or background, you will need to make some important decisions.

Color Schemes

The colors you decide to use in your Round Robin quilt are purely your preference. Use colors that fit into your decorating scheme, or find ones that you think look pretty together. If you have a place in mind to hang the finished quilt, think about the colors used in the room. Let them influence your color scheme. Look outside for inspiration. Mother Nature paints some beautiful color combinations in large and small places. Maybe a sheet of gift wrap or a special greeting card will spark an idea. Who knows what color combinations will catch your eye? Trust your own color sense, even if you think no one else will like it. This is to be your quilt and you are the one who will live with it when it is finished.

Themes

Selecting a theme is an easy way to unify and coordinate all Round Robin projects. Do you want the focus to be a special event, such as a golden wedding anniversary? You might use lots of yellow. Patriotic themes suggest red, white, and blue combinations. What about a holiday theme centered around Christmas or Valentine's Day? The seasons of spring, summer, autumn, and winter all bring color schemes, fabrics, and motifs to mind. Maybe a whimsy will strike your fancy and your quilt will make us smile.

In addition, think about moods and feelings. Do you want your quilt to be dignified, formal, elegant? What about a serene and calm feeling? Bright colors can be joyful and uplifting or they can be beautiful and rich, like jewel tones. Subtle, muted colors are usually more restful and peaceful.

Fabric Selection

We prefer and recommend fabrics that are 100% cotton. They have a softer look than synthetics and blends and are easier to handle, especially when doing appliqué.

Make sure your palette of fabrics has enough contrast for differentiation between shapes, borders, and motifs, so necessary for a successful design. You can accomplish this by selecting fabrics with a good balance of lights, mediums, and darks. Also, include some values that are close together so that you can do some gradual shading if desired.

Use prints of all sizes—small, medium, and large. This adds texture and interest to the quilt. In the Add-On Appliqué projects, you will use mostly small- and medium-scale prints.

Instead of using large quantities of two or three coordinated fabrics for the color scheme, try using smaller amounts of many coordinated fabrics. We like to follow the words of friend, author, and quiltmaker Margaret Miller, who says, "Why use two fabrics when you can use twenty!" When trying to reintroduce a fabric, color, or value in another area of the quilt, you don't always need to duplicate the exact same print that appeared previously. Finding another fabric that is the same, or nearly the same, color is not only challenging but also makes the quilt less predictable. If the owner is lucky, someone will find the perfect print that contains several of the colors used in the quilt. This fabric helps unify and coordinate the project. Buy lots of it!

When working on these projects, it is usually fun and challenging to work with color palettes and fabrics selected by other quilters. It is interesting to see the combinations people have chosen. Your ideas about color and creativity are stretched and expanded. Occasionally, a project will come to you that has colors you have never used before and probably will never use again! Remind yourself that we are all different and we each have our own sense of color. Be glad your time with this particular color scheme is short! Who knows? You might even learn to like these colors a little. Won't you be surprised when a small amount of that icky green finds its way into your next quilt?

Pack the Travel Bag

Each participant prepares a special box or bag for the project to travel through the rotations. Some people enjoy finding boxes appropriate to the theme of the project. Others decorate special boxes for this purpose. A clean, unused pizza box, covered with fabric or gift wrap, is one option.

Place the project inside the box along with a journal, fabrics, and other items allowed by the group guidelines. See "Items to Include in the Owner's Box" on pages 16–17. It is a good idea to put your name and telephone number on the outside of the box. Put your box under your arm and head for the meeting place. You are ready for take-off!

In Flight (The First Exchange)

When you all meet on the appointed day, the rotation begins. It is fun to get together so everyone can see the beginning of each project. The variety will be amazing! While looking at all the projects, participants start getting ideas they might be able to use when it is "their turn." Bring your cameras to this meeting. It is fun to take pictures of the projects at the very beginning to compare with the final results—"before" and "after" photos for the journals. Take photographs of individuals with their projects and a group shot as well.

The projects, as they are passed around, are like a painter's canvas, where the owner starts the painting and other participants use their imaginations and fabric palettes to contribute to the overall beauty of the painting. We each have a different sense of color, different ideas about design, and different interests in quiltmaking, not to mention life in general. What fun it is to see the personalities, uniqueness, and humor that each of your friends stitch into each project! Janie will use red if she can, Terry will try to include flamingos, and Kathleen will always find a special paisley print to use.

The individual additions made by participants are like different instruments in the orchestra, each with its own tune and part to play. How beautiful it is when they all play in harmony in your project!

At each meeting, it is helpful to ask how things are going. If a technique is troubling someone, plan a mini-workshop or demonstration. All the members can benefit from seeing and hearing different ways of doing things.

If your group plans to have show-and-tell at each rotation meeting, it's a good idea to record the progress of each block with snapshots. One group did this and placed the resulting Polaroid shots in the respective boxes so there was a visual record with each project.

Coming in for the Landing

After all the rotations are completed, plan a special unveiling event. A special "hanging" or exhibition is fun. Decide on a date when all the quilts will be totally completed and plan a reunion. Show-and-tell at this event is a celebration of creativity. Borders frame the medallion Round Robin quilts like a painting. Quilting designs bring the themes of the Add-On Appliqué and Around-the-Block quilts to life. The backs of the quilts and the labels reflect the themes of the fronts.

The common thread that brings the participants together is their love of quiltmaking. Their time together nourishes the need for contact with others. The finished product is the result of cooperative efforts, learning, and creativity. Looking at each quilt is a reminder of the gift of friendship.

"The camaraderie we shared during the making of this quilt was wonderful. Besides the fun and fellowship we experienced every time our group met, there seemed to exist a special bonding of the quilt-group members as the quilt itself was 'bonded' together."

Chris Mewhinney

"I have since moved from the area. The quilt will forever remind me of the closeness I had with the Material Girls. They are more than just a quilt group—they are friends who appreciate chocolate and good wine, who also don't have perfect kids, who have to reintroduce their husbands to a vacuum cleaner, and who made me laugh."

Janine Lauderback

Border Beauties

Medallion Friendship Quilts

Variety
People and patchwork
stitched together with love
warm and comforting
        Haiku by Anna Brown

Medallion quilts are beautiful. They have a center block, "the medallion," surrounded by several borders, each designed as a "frame" that enhances the overall effect of the quilt. Medallion quilts are a natural format for Round Robin friendship quilts. The Presentation quilts of the early nineteenth century were often organized this way. A center block was made to celebrate a special event, to honor a special person or place, or to showcase a beautiful technique or idea. Borders were then concentrically built around the theme square. It is said that Martha Washington made a medallion quilt in 1790 to commemorate William Penn's 1683 treaty with the Indians. Later, medallion quilts were made to recognize the inauguration of presidents or to commemorate the signing of documents proclaiming statehood. Today, we may choose to create a medallion that is also a commemoration—of a special event or of a special friendship.

The Border Beauties Process

The Border Beauties quilt project begins with all participants making a center theme block. These are then passed on in a predesignated rotation order, with each participant adding a border that follows the project guidelines. On the appointed date, the projects move on to the next person, who adds another border. This continues until each participant has added to each block except the one they started. Everyone ends up with a quilt top composed of their original block surrounded by borders made by different friends. The owner then finishes the quilt.

This concept is believed to have originated in Bolingbrook, Illinois, by Patti Miller, when she and some of her quilting friends formed a Round Robin–type group.

Border Beauties Guidelines

Using the following information as a guide, develop the project guidelines, then distribute them to all participants. Be sure to include: names, addresses, telephone numbers, general guidelines, rotation order and dates, as well as the type of borders to add on each round.

Group Size

A group of four to six quilters works best for this style of Round Robin project. The number of people in the group determines the number of borders. This also becomes a factor in the size of the project.

Project Size

Consider the approximate finished quilt size. This will help determine the approximate size of the center block. Do you want to make wall quilts or bed quilts? Consider the number of borders and their approximate width as well.

Determine the size of the center block to be used. It can be one size for everyone, for example, 12" square, or the makers can be given a range, such as between 12"–15" square. The most common sizes for center blocks made by most groups are in the 12"–18" range. If you're doing a miniature, of course, you must start with a much smaller center block!

Types of Borders

Define the border challenge and the criteria to be used for each rotation. Some groups do not set any special rules for the addition of each border. Their philosophy is to be creative and "whatever happens, happens." Most groups challenge the participants by indicating certain criteria to be used for each rotation and border. See "Sample Group Guidelines" on pages 32–38 for border themes and rules. Notice the variety of borders in the photographs of the medallion-style quilts in this book. Use them for inspiration.

Different techniques as well as themes can be chosen for specific borders, for example:

Rotation 1 (Border 1). Use a pattern composed of triangles.

Rotation 2 (Border 2). Set the block with the first border on point and add a border composed of squares and/or rectangles.

Rotation 3 (Border 3). Add a border with an appliquéd design.

Rotation 4 (Border 4). Use a pattern with points.

The experience and skill level of group members help determine the types of borders selected for the project. If the group does not have a lot of quiltmaking experience, keep border designs simple and achieve variety through the use of color and fabric. If the group has mastered more advanced techniques, try including a border that requires curves or appliqué. Some groups add a theme border that reflects the personality of the quilt owner or one that depicts the area where she lives.

When borders are selected, think about the order in which they will be added to the project and plan accordingly. For example, an appliqué border might need to be added early in the project before the borders get too big.

Border Width

Some groups prefer to set a range of width sizes for the borders. This helps eliminate the rapid growth in size that can occur when wide borders are added during the rotations.

The width of each border will vary, depending upon the units and motifs selected by the maker. Be sure the border designs have enough freedom and flexibility to be fluid and to turn gracefully around the corners.

Gracious Generosity by Lorna Flack Druffel, 1993, Colton, Washington, 54" x 54". Lorna's friends created the illusion of curves and a flowing design, which is enhanced by quilting in the open areas.

The Material Girls (the name for one Round Robin group) used a different method to keep their quilts from growing too large. Each participant added borders to only two sides of the quilt. This gave variety to the borders, and their quilts have an interesting and unique look to them. The Material Girls and their quilts are pictured on pages 36–37.

Rotation Order and Time Schedule

The amount of time between rotations depends upon the size of the end product, the difficulty of each border, and the schedules of all the participants. As the borders are added to the center block, the quilt becomes larger and more time is needed to accomplish the task. The types of borders selected also determine the length of time between rotations. If holidays fall in the time frame, add extra time for these rotations.

Adequate time results in a better quilt. A month is usually an adequate amount of time to finish a pieced border. More complex borders, such as those that require appliqué or curved edges, may require two months between rotations.

Show-and-Tell

Consider the options discussed under "Guidelines for All Groups" on pages 13–15.

Items to Include in the Owner's Box

See pages 16–17 for detailed information about items the owner can include in the project box with the center block before passing it on. Also, refer to your own group guidelines.

Owner's Options

The group needs to make a decision regarding how much the owner can change or add to the quilt after it is returned to them. Can one more border be added if needed? Can appliqué be added over existing borders?

Mini-Workshops

Mini-workshops or technique demonstrations are very valuable. Now is the time to think about where they would fit into the schedule if they are needed.

Reunion Party

Plan to have a time for show-and-tell when all the projects have been assembled and quilted. Refer to page 15 for more information.

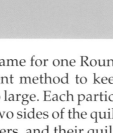

Living in a Material World by Cynthia Stroo, 1993, Duvall, Washington, 39" x 41". Members of the Material Girls added borders to only two sides of their quilts to give them a unique asymmetrical appearance. This one has a folk-art look.

Border Basics for Medallion Quilts

Medallion quilts are unique. Most traditional quilts have a certain number of blocks that can be set together in a variety of ways. The medallion quilt features a theme block with a variety of borders framing the center panel. While the owner of the quilt may have a basic idea or plan for this type of quilt, these quilts often build themselves as each border is added and the design progresses outward.

Medallion quilts look complicated and overwhelming, and quiltmakers are often afraid these quilts are beyond their capabilities. Quilters shy away from them because they are afraid that the math required to make perfectly fitting borders is more than they want to tackle. Or, they think their designing skills are not sharp enough to create borders that flow gracefully around the corners. Still others are afraid that the finished quilt will not lie flat. You can banish all of these concerns by using the tips and hints that follow. "Border Beauties" should be fun—not agony.

Repetition

One of the most important secrets for a successful medallion quilt is repetition. Repeating color, fabrics, and/or designs relates the various parts of the quilt to each other and creates a feeling of continuity. Your border addition may not be the place to add something new and exciting to someone's project. Put away those ideas for fancy, elaborate designs you've always wanted to try and challenge yourself to repeat and rearrange shapes, to reintroduce fabrics already used, and to

Bordering on Friendship by Nancy J. Martin, 1993, Woodinville, Washington, 64" x 64". Nancy's friends knew of her love of pastels, floral prints, buttons, charms, and other assorted items, and matched the quilt to her personality.

> "It was a great challenge to always add a border that met the requirements of our Round Robin and enhanced the flavor of the quilt without taking over as the center of interest."
>
> *Kathy White*

use colors in new ways in your border addition. Look for ways to carry out the theme of the quilt. Keep the owner's ideas and colors in mind.

Color Schemes, Themes, and Fabric Selection

First read the basic information on pages 18 and 86–94. As you select fabrics, be sure to include a dark-value fabric in the center as well as in the outermost border to make the quilt visually pleasing to the eye. Darker fabrics serve as an anchor for the center block and help prevent the illusion of a hole in the center of the design. When the dark value is again repeated in the outermost border or binding, it serves as a frame to contain the design and keeps the eye from wandering off the edges of the quilt.

Theme (Center) Block

You may wish to make a new theme block specifically for your Border Beauties quilt, or you might already have a single block that is especially nice and worthy of being framed by multiple borders.

The center block is the focus of the quilt. It should be the star attraction and say, "Hey, look at me—I'm special!" Visually, it needs to be prominent and strong, capable of standing alone and certainly worthy of framing. It is the place to spotlight the theme and color scheme. It is the focal point that will draw observers to come and spend more time studying the quilt. Colors and fabrics, shapes and motifs introduced in the center block should be repeated in the borders all the way to the outermost edges of the quilt.

The center block can be simple or elaborate. Pieced blocks, such as star patterns, Mariner's Compass, and picture blocks are good choices. Even a simple star with an unusual fabric or motif spotlighted in the center is an easy way to get started. Appliqué blocks of the Baltimore Album type, folk-art style designs, or blocks with realistic motifs and landscapes also work well.

Think about themes—holiday, Oriental, or patriotic, for example.

If you begin with a simple design, make it exciting by using a beautiful piece of fabric you've been saving for a special quilt, or create a smashing color scheme that needs simple lines to keep the design from appearing busy and confusing. Notice how the center block in "Bordering on Friendship" effectively shows off a beautiful floral fabric.

If you want to use a more elaborate design, pick one that will show off fancy techniques you've been practicing. You can piece the block, use appliqué, or combine both techniques. If you have time, make the block a little more complex than the average pattern. An elaborate Feathered Star block is featured in the center of "Six Stars All A Round." It is the center of attraction and sets the theme for the entire quilt.

There is no general rule for the finished size of the quilt or how large the theme or center block should be. Neither is there a rule about how many borders or what percentage of the quilt surface they should cover. The theme block must be large enough to make a statement; it is the subject of the quilt. The borders should enhance the center design, make it sparkle, and play a supportive role.

Patterns for seven appropriate center blocks begin on page 39, but the design possibilities are endless.

Getting Started

In the medallion quilt, the theme block is surrounded by numerous borders or frames. The main purpose of any border in this type of quilt is to enhance the center design and reflect its beauty. The borders should relate to the center block by echoing some of its colors, fabrics, shapes, and theme ideas. This creates continuity and helps to achieve a harmonious, coordinated design.

The framelike borders should play a subordinate role and not stand out or overwhelm the center. The borders of medallion

Six Stars All A Round by Kathy L. Marks, 1993, Hayden Lake, Idaho, 65" x 85". Kathy's friends used stars of different sizes to unify this beautiful quilt.

quilts often look complicated, and some of them are complex, but the majority of them are simple variations of themes, shapes, motifs, colors, and fabrics used in or inspired by the center block.

Border Design Inspiration

When you receive a project, take it out of its box and place it on a wall. It helps to see the overall design when the quilt is in a vertical position. Think about the theme and using the colors, units, and motifs to carry the ideas from the center block outward. Let ideas percolate as the quilt speaks to you. Keep the owner in mind as you plan the border. Be sensitive to the choice of colors and the mood of the design. Plan to add borders that are appropriate rather than focusing on designing the most beautiful border in the world. For border ideas, look through some of the books listed in the "Bibliography" on page 128. Study the photographs and illustrations in this book, too, for ideas. Consider the border designs on this page and on pages 26–31. Sketch your ideas or put them on graph paper.

Consider the following as you plan and execute border designs:

- Border designs are composed of basic units (blocks) that are repeated to make long rows that fit the sides of the quilt. Units can be pieced, appliquéd, or made using a combination of both techniques.
- Each border should flow smoothly around the quilt. This is accomplished by giving special attention to the corners.
- The border can be simple or elaborate. When necessary, keep the design simple. A border that is too elaborate or too busy will detract from the beauty of the project.
- Repetition of shapes found in the theme (center) block gives continuity to the total design.

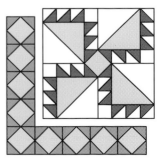

- Sometimes you can fracture the theme-block design and use sections of it in one of the borders.

- Don't be afraid to change the background fabrics throughout the medallion. Some borders can have a light background while others can have a darker background. The variety makes the quilt more interesting.

Border 1

Border 2

- Vary the color use in each border. A color may be used prominently in one border but only serve as an accent in another border. Change the proportions of colors used in the various borders to create more interest. *Do not choose a totally new color scheme for a border. Always stick with the same colors established in the theme block.* It is OK to introduce new fabrics with these same colors, though.
- Consider using a fabric that is almost, but not quite, the same as one that was previously used. Just a little difference or variation can lend subtle texture to the entire quilt. Turn the fabric over to see if the back side is appropriate. Sometimes this side is more muted and lighter in value than the front and is just what you need.

⑤ Use a variety of techniques in different borders. Appliqué softens the strong, straight lines of piecing. Curved piecing is a nice alternative and accomplishes the same thing. Don't forget that a plain border is an interesting change and provides a wonderful backdrop for whole-cloth quilting designs that repeat previously used shapes, themes, or motifs. When working on a friend's project, *it takes courage to add a simple border to a quilt instead of using your best ideas and skills.* In the end, that person will thank you for thinking of the overall scheme of things and adding to the beauty of the quilt by inserting a quiet place in the design.

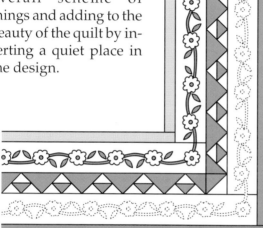

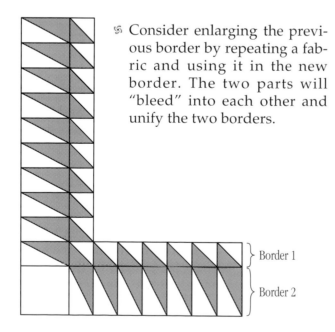

⑤ Consider enlarging the previous border by repeating a fabric and using it in the new border. The two parts will "bleed" into each other and unify the two borders.

Border 1

Border 2

✑ Tip

Before making borders for all sides of the quilt, make one border and place it next to the unfinished quilt top.

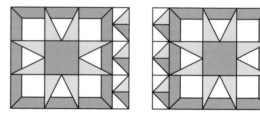

If the border design is asymmetrical (uneven), try placing both long sides next to the unfinished quilt top. Each side will have a different effect when placed next to the edge of the quilt top. Which way looks best? For both symmetrical and asymmetrical borders, check to be sure the seams match and the overall design is pleasing to the eye. Make adjustments, if necessary, then make borders for the three other sides.

Once you have an idea for a border, it is time to actually design the basic unit. Use graph paper or sketch your ideas. Start by drawing several designs or parts of designs. Use both ends of your pencil as you work. The sharp end of the pencil adds new lines and creates shapes. The eraser deletes lines and creates open spaces that enhance the designs you are creating. Let the ideas flow. It is helpful to generate a lot of ideas and go through a weeding-out process rather than trying to come up with just one idea. Keep a notebook of ideas. If one doesn't work in a project, it may be the inspiration for your next quilt.

When introducing a new element, remember to integrate it with the overall design. For example, if the project has been pieced up to the point you receive it, and the next border calls for appliqué, coordinate the angles and curves, perhaps by repeating fabrics from another border or even combining these two techniques.

Border Engineering

We wish we could give you a magic formula for selecting border designs and units, or a rule for determining how wide to make the borders so proportion and balance are perfect. We wish there were magic wands to wave over the designs to make them come out even so they turn the corners gracefully and have no problems meeting and matching. Instead, we can tell you that designing the borders is not as difficult as it seems if you plan ahead and use some basic mathematics.

Pat seems to like the mathematical part of the design process. At least, it doesn't become a major hurdle for her as she plans a project. Some quilters will be like Pat. However, if you are like Donna, you do not have a lot of confidence in your ability to do any kind of math. You think of math as the "M" word and use numbers for figuring only when necessary. Of course, some of you will be a combination of both types of people. If you are like Donna, it may be necessary to have a conversation with yourself right now. Say, "Self, remember all persons are not good at math. But I want to do the best job I can on my friends' projects. So, I will always use correct measurements, plan carefully, and do the best job I can. I might use more math than I have used in a year, but I want to avoid mistakes. The time I spend in careful planning now will be time well spent."

Pat prefers to design all her borders on graph paper first. She is then more confident about how they will look when completed. One square on the graph paper is the equivalent of a specific measurement. Usually, she assigns one square of graph paper to represent one square inch of a true-life quilt. After she has a line drawing of her border design, she places tracing paper over the top and tries different color schemes and value-placement options. The paper is transparent, so she never has to redraw her lines. After analyzing the colorations and comparing them to the unfinished quilt top, she finds it easier to make a decision and choose the option that works best.

Definitions

Before you start your trial border designs, it is helpful to understand the following terminology.

Unit: One part of the border design. Units can be very simple or very complex.

Unit Size: The length of one unit design. Square units may be 3" x 3" or 4" x 4", for example.

Rectangular units might be 1½" x 5".

Unit Repeats: Units placed next to each other like blocks in a row to make the border the correct length.

Corner Unit: The unit that connects the side borders so the design turns and flows gracefully around the quilt. The corners can be the same as a border unit, or they might be a different, but coordinating design.

Plain Narrow Border: An unpieced border that serves as a "spacer" or "filler." Use one to add length to the quilt to make the math part of the designing process easier. Try a plain border to separate two busy borders. If this narrow strip is the same color as the background, it causes the design to "float."

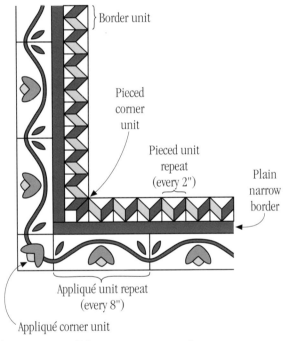

Accurate Measurements

As the quilt top grows, it is essential that each person use accurate measurements as the basis for all designing. Accurate measurements must be taken each step along the way. If mistakes are made now, they are only compounded later.

One of the most important measurements is the finished size of the quilt top after each border is added. Many quilters mistakenly measure the outside edges of the quilt while it is lying flat. The raw edges of the quilt may have stretched during the sewing and pressing process. The resulting figures are a s-t-r-e-t-c-h-e-d measurement and are inaccurate. If these figures are used to cut the border strips, the border will ruffle and will not lie flat.

are used to cut the border strips, the border will ruffle and will not lie flat.

To obtain an accurate measurement, always measure through the center of the quilt top. Measure the horizontal distance to obtain the length of the top and bottom borders. Take the vertical measurement through the center of the quilt to determine the length of the side borders. These measurements determine the length of the new border.

In spite of our best efforts, there is some-

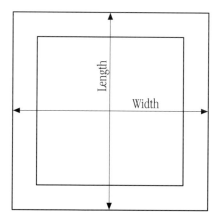

times as much as 1"–6" difference between the measurements taken through the center of the quilt and the measurements of the outer edges. When this happens, make the necessary corrections by following the instructions for easing on page 31 in the section on "Fudging to Fit." *Correct the problem now; otherwise it will only get worse as the quilt top grows.*

Unit Size/Quilt Relationship

For perfect-fitting borders, the size of the border unit should relate to the size of the theme block or unfinished quilt and should be a number that you can divide into the quilt-top di-

mension equally. For example, if you are adding the first border to a theme block that measures 18" x 18", you can use a border unit that measures 3" x 3". If you divide 18 by 3, you will need

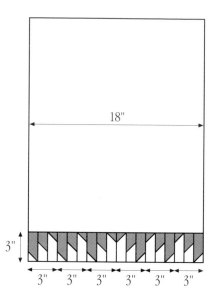

6 repeat units for each side of the block. A fraction of a unit will not work.

The size of the repeat does not necessarily need to be in whole inches. Fractions (but not less than ½") are OK. For example, on a quilt top that measures 27" x 27" (unfinished), you could use 6 repeat units that are 4½" long (27 divided by 4½"= 6).

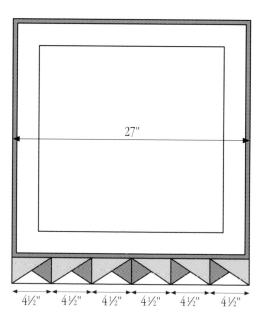

Spacer Border

If the block or quilt-top measurement will *not* divide evenly, consider adding a plain (unpieced) narrow border before adding the new border. Plan it so the width of the spacer strip brings the quilt to a measurement that can be evenly divided by the size of the unit.

To find the width of the spacer border, take the length of the border to be added and subtract the length of the quilt top. Divide this number by 2. This is the finished width of the spacer border needed for each side of the quilt. The formula is:

$$\frac{\text{Border length - Quilt-top length}}{2} = \begin{array}{l}\text{finished width of} \\ \text{spacer border}\end{array}$$

Add ½" for seam allowances to this figure to determine the cut width of the spacer border strip.

For example, if you are adding a 28"-long border and the quilt-top measurement is 26½", you would cut the spacer strips 1¼" wide.

28" - 26½" = 1½" ÷ 2 = 3/4" + ½" = 1¼" (cut width for spacer strip)

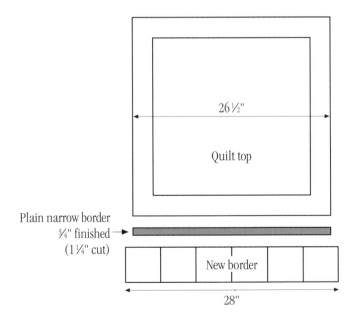

Plain narrow border
¾" finished →
(1¼" cut)

The narrow border also serves other purposes. If the fabric for the narrow border you are adding is the same as one of the fabrics in the border next to it, the design will "float."

If you use a contrasting fabric or color, then a narrow border serves as a frame or edging that separates two busy areas.

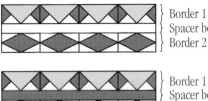

} Border 1
} Spacer border (floater)
} Border 2

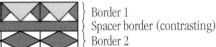

} Border 1
} Spacer border (contrasting)
} Border 2

If the borders will be placed side by side without a spacer border, it is visually preferable to have a mathematical relationship between the units of both borders. If there is no visual relationship of unit sizes between borders, points and seams will not match and the borders will look askew.

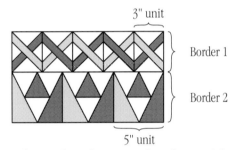

If you decide to use borders without a common mathematical factor after all, try inserting a spacer border between them. It will put distance between these irregularities and make the transition appear more natural and pleasing.

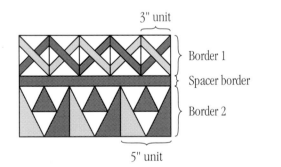

When units are the same size in both borders, seams match, points line up, and the units end at the same place at the corners.

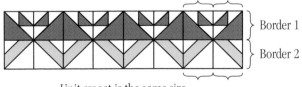

} Border 1
} Border 2

Unit repeat is the same size
in both borders.

Seams also match when one of the border units is a multiple of the other. For example, if one border has a 6" unit, the adjacent border could have a 2" or 3" unit size.

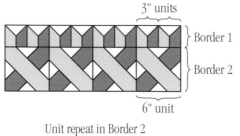

Unit repeat in Border 2
is a multiple size of Border 1.

Corner Units

Borders should turn the corners smoothly and gracefully. They act as an effective frame that allows the eye to move around and across the quilt without interruption. A corner block that does not continue the flow of the repeated border units gives an unbalanced look not only to the border but to the entire quilt. Therefore, pay special attention to the corner design so that it flows easily.

Some designs turn corners nicely with just another unit block added at the corners. This means the design simply goes to the corner and then turns to go around the next edge.

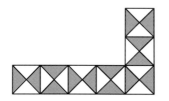

Mitering the corner unit is another way to produce a design that turns a smooth corner.

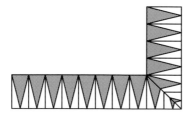

Some borders turn nicely with a plain block in the corner.

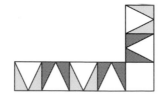

If the border unit is directional or asymmetrical, you can reverse its direction in the middle of each side border. If there is an even number of repeats per side, the reversal will take place with one-half of the repeats going one way and the other half going in the other direction.

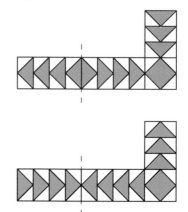

Even number of repeats

If there is an odd number of asymmetrical units in each side of the border, you may need to change the center unit to something different. Reverse the direction of the units on both sides of the dissimilar block. This new center block can also be placed in the corner for a unifying effect.

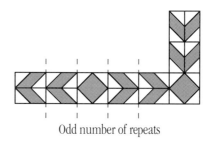

Odd number of repeats

You can change or modify the border unit to create the corner-unit design. In this case, the border units end at the corner. Whenever new elements or ideas are introduced, remember to design corners that turn naturally and keep the borders flowing continuously.

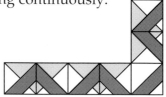

Appliqué borders are treated in the same manner. The size of the repeat should be related to the block or quilt measurement. One way to determine the size of the units is to take a piece of paper that is the length and width of the finished border, fold it into even divisions, and treat each division as a unit. Use this unit size when designing the appliqué motifs.

If the appliqué border design has vines, you can end the vine anywhere in the border and use a different design in the corner.

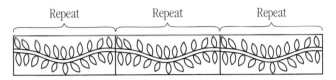

Fudging to Fit

Sometimes you cannot add a new border directly to the last border of the quilt and have the two come together evenly. Perhaps the new border is too long or short to fit the quilt top. What happens when the quilt does not arrive at your home perfectly square? Since we are human quilters and do not make perfect quilts or perfect borders in spite of our best intentions and strict attention to detail, it is almost certain that somewhere during the rotation cycle, someone will receive a quilt that will need some adjustments before the next round of borders can be added. Don't panic when any of these things happens to you. This section is for you!

Take time right now to pour yourself another cup of coffee or glass of lemonade. Take a deep breath. The necessary adjustments must be made now or the problems will only be compounded as each new border is added.

The first step is to analyze and identify the problem. Why won't the new border fit? Is it too long? Too short? Does the border have lots of points that will require extra-careful precision piecing to match them to your pieced border? There are two solutions that solve most of the problems encountered when adding multiple borders to a quilt: easing or using a fudging border.

Easing. Use this technique when the measurement of one or more of the outside edges of the quilt is not the same as the true measurement through the center of the quilt. See "Accurate Measurments" on pages 27–28. You can gently ease in the extra fullness of these edges so they will fit the border being added. Be sure you have measured accurately and that the length of the new border is accurate.

Determine the halfway point on the edge of the quilt as show in the illustration below; pin or mark. Find the halfway point on the border strip you are adding. Next, find the quarter points on the edge of the quilt and the new border; pin the two borders together at these points. Continue to pin the borders to the quilt top, easing in the extra fullness so there are no tucks or puckers. Sew carefully, gently easing any extra fullness as necessary. It helps to sew with the eased edge against the feed dog of the sewing machine.

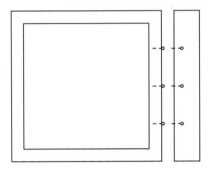

Fudging Border. This unpieced little border can hide a multitude of sins! It is the same as the plain narrow border described on page 29. Use it to help with the following problems:

- ⑤ There are many points in the previous border and you are not sure you can make them all match the units in the new border precisely. Add a fudging strip first.
- ⑤ The new border is too long. Lengthen the quilt top by adding a fudging border that brings the dimensions of the previous border to the proper size.

Problem Solving: Other Ideas

When you receive a Round Robin project, you may encounter one or more of these challenges.

- ⑤ The quilt arrives at your doorstep and there is a problem that can't be fixed by easing or using a narrow fudging border.
- ⑤ Major resewing is needed because piecing has not been done precisely and intersections do not match.
- ⑤ There are points that will not be sharp because they are much farther or closer than

¼" from the edge of the fabric. When a new border is added, some of the points will be chopped off while others will be miles away from the seam.

ఌ A motif is not appliquéd well and is not secure.

These are all real problems that have been experienced by Round Robin quiltmakers.

If the problems are serious and happen often, perhaps workshops and demonstrations should be planned to help all participants learn more about precision piecing, appliqué methods, and other techniques. Regular encouragement to do a job well is also helpful.

If someone's workmanship is just not up to basic standards or if there is a major design problem, then there are no easy answers. This is a difficult situation. For friendship's sake, we suggest you tread softly and carefully. The person probably thought the project was OK since it was passed along. The person who receives the quilt sees it differently. The project now needs adjustments before another border can be added.

After careful thought, you may decide it is necessary to speak to the person who added the last border. If so, keep in mind that some people take suggestions well while others take them personally. If the problem is one of design, perhaps you can design the new border so that the approach becomes a collaborative effort between you and the other person, with both of you working toward the integration and coordination of the two borders.

If you decide to say nothing and serious adjustments have to be made, do not become bogged down or discouraged. Allow yourself to whine twice a day in the privacy of your own home. Then try to treat the quilt as if it were one of your own. (No, you can't just put it in a box and forget it.) Think of this as an opportunity to practice creativity and put your problem-solving skills to work. By the time you find the solution to the problem, make the adjustments, do the necessary sewing, and then add your own border, you'll be ready to give yourself a pat on the back and treat yourself to some real fudge!

Finishing the Project

After the rotations are complete, each quilt top returns to its owner. Some quilt tops obviously need one more border as a final frame and others are ready to be layered into a quilt sandwich and quilted. Information on selecting borders and quilting designs appears on pages 95–97. Refer to pages 101–15 for quilt-finishing techniques.

The Border Beauties format is a fun and exciting friendship experience. By the time your quilt is completed, you will be a "Medallion Master," a "First Fiddle Framer," and a "Proficient Perimeter Professional."

Sample Group Guidelines

Monday Night Bowling League
Seattle, Washington

This group of quilters is a satellite group of Quilters Anonymous, the largest guild in the Seattle area. They divided into three smaller groups to work on Round Robin projects.

Round Robin Rules

1. Treat each growing quilt with great respect. Keep the quilt in a clean, dry place. Protect the quilt from direct sunlight. Have a special, specific place to keep the quilt so that it does not disappear in a messy studio.
2. Prewash each and every fabric that you add to the quilt. Test each fabric to be certain that it is colorfast.
3. Sew with care to match points and corners. Do your best to make the craftsmanship on the quilt perfect.
4. Press gently. Replace the quilt in the box and bring it to the Bowling League or deliver it to the next person on the list as promptly as you can.

Round Robin Design Challenges

Add to the center block in the order below.

1. **Triangles**. Attach a 2"- to 3"-wide border made of half-square and/or quarter-square triangles. You can use one triangle, a few triangles, or an entire border of triangles. It's your decision.

2. **Squares and rectangles**. Turn the bordered block on point and add a 2"- to 4"-wide border, including some squares and rectangles. When you turn the block on point, you can piece the corner (filler) triangles, you can appliqué something on the corner triangles, or you can leave them plain. It's your decision.

3. **Northwest**. Create a border of 3" to 6" blocks or portions of blocks that include birds, trees, mountains, water, wind, or rain in the block name. (I can just picture several of us flagrantly renaming these blocks.)

4. **Friendship**. Add a 3"- to 6"-wide pieced border, including some element that reflects the center block maker's personality, tastes, lifestyle, and/or interests.

5. **Points**. Complete the quilt top by attaching a 2"- to 6"-wide border that includes points. Again, you can choose the type of points, the number, and the direction in which they point. (Several of you have asked me to specify not to use Prairie Points.)

Some of the Bowling League Quiltmakers are pictured with quilts in the group photo below. Nancy J. Martin's quilt, *Bordering on Friendship*, is shown on page 23.

These members of the Monday Night Bowling League, Seattle, Washington, proudly display their Border Beauties Round Robin quilts. (Nancy J. Martin, Joan Dawson, Kathy White, Laura Reinstatler, and Diane Coombs)

Out to Lunch Bunch
Coeur d'Alene, Idaho

"I don't think I have ever suffered more over a quilt project in my life! But the personal growth was well worth the effort. Our group as a whole had excellent quiltmaking skills. I think it was very important to be at the same level of expertise."
Jean VanBockel

The former owners and employees of a fabric shop wanted to continue their friendship and share their love of quilting with each other after the shop closed. Twelve members meet once each month. Six of these quilters branched out to try the Round Robin experience. Kathy White, a member of the Monday Night Bowling League, shared her group's rules with the Out to Lunch Bunch. One of its members, Jean VanBockel, is Kathy's sister.

Members met once a month for breakfast and to exchange projects. After the final rotation, the quilters and their spouses gathered at a summer potluck, where the projects were returned to their owners. As they enjoyed their feast, they admired the exhibit of quilt tops, which were hanging on a l-o-n-g clothesline!

Round Robin Rules

1. General rules are the same as for the Monday Night Bowling League. (See pages 32–33.)
2. Make the center block 14"–18" square.
3. Include 1 yard of fabric in the box.
4. Include a 4" x 6" index card in your box with a little about yourself—likes and dislikes, favorite things, and information about your family. (This was particularly helpful for the friendship round.)

Quiltmakers who participated in this project are: Thine Lu Bloxham, *Voyager* (page 52); Pam Bryceson, *Bejeweled* (page 51); Kathy L. Marks, *Six Stars All A Round* (page 24); Gayle Noyes, *All My Quilting Friends Are Stars* (page 55); Ardell Powers Parkin, *To Market to Market* (page 53); Jean VanBockel, *Midnight Sunflower* (page 53)

A Group of Friends
Lacey, Washington

"We all worked to design something that would integrate with other borders to make the quilt look as if it were made by one person. It pushed me to be more creative. These projects gave me confidence. If I could do it in a group, I could to it on my own!"
Dotti Wilke

This is a relaxed group of friends. They wanted to make sure their Round Robin experience would be a fun project with collaboration and positive feelings. They wanted to incorporate the colors and designs used in the center block and kept that in the back of their minds as they searched for ideas and solutions to design challenges.

None of them wanted to work in a vacuum, so they vetoed the "keeping-things-secret" approach and met for show-and-tell each time the quilts were exchanged. This gave them a chance to share ideas and make suggestions. Their four strong egos would not be denied, and they were not afraid to bend the rules or take criticism.

They probably all worked harder on these quilts than they would have on their own projects. Working on a friend's quilt proved to be scary but exciting. They stretched their imaginations, and since they had to work with "strange" colors, their stash of fabrics grew. They polished their math to make sure their designs fit the space for which it was intended. Quilt books were dusted off in search of ideas and there was a good bit of agonizing once a decision was made. (Will she like it?) They always felt free to bounce any ideas off each other and usually went their own way despite some good advice.

Round Robin Rules

1. The owner makes a square with no criteria attached.
2. Round 1: Turn the square on point and add a piecework border.
3. Round 2: Appliqué
4. Round 3: Triangles

Quiltmakers who participated in this project were: Ute Jarasitis, *I Can't Believe It's Mine!* (page 52); Rachel Nichols, *Old-Fashioned Star* (Sara Rea, owner) (page 47); Sara Quattlebaum, *Magenta Magic* (page 48); Dotti Wilke, *Black and White and Red All Over* (page 48).

"Every time the blocks were revealed, it was like opening brand new Christmas packages! Each round seemed so right and so creative. How flattering it was to have each person put so much energy into my quilt!"

Marta Estes

BUMM'S (K) Rush
Woodinville, Washington

"The idea of sewing for each special person, thinking of what they would want while still giving it our imprint was challenging and lots of fun. The beauty of quilting is being 'connected' with the recipient during the process, drawing you closer in friendship!"

Marion Shelton

This group of co-workers at That Patchwork Place decided to start a progressive quilt after seeing some of the Monday Night Bowling League Round Robin quilts. The Bumm's (K) Rush grew out of "Run for the Border" as Round Robin quilts are called in Texas. They added the initials of their first names and came up with the Bumm's Rush. The (K) was added during the second rotation when Kerry joined the group. (Their rules appear on page 36.)

Participants made their blocks in March 1993 and unveiled their quilt tops at a company meeting in October 1993. They kept this project

The BUMM'S (K) RUSH ladies kept their Border Beauties Round Robin quilt projects secret from the owners and used the "no rules" philosophy. The final results show a variety of beautiful designs. (Bottom row: Barbara Weiland and Kerry I. Hoffman, middle row: Marion L. Shelton and Marta Estes, back row: Ursula Reikes and Susan I. Jones)

a complete secret from co-workers for eight months—a feat in itself! As a result of the showing, another Round Robin group of co-workers formed within a week.

Blocks were rotated at a lunch on the first Wednesday of each month. Because Kerry joined after the first round, the rotation was adjusted slightly and she had to do some fast stitching. At the end of the rotation, two participants had two quilt tops requiring borders in the same month. An extra month was added to the schedule to help them out.

Because there were no rules to follow for each round, the size and shape of the resulting quilt tops is quite varied.

Round Robin Rules

1. Make a 12" (finished) block in the design of your choice.
2. Pass the block, following the rotation (BUMMSK).
3. You may consult with each other about what to add to the growing quilt top, but keep everything secret from the owner.
4. The only other rule is that there are no rules. Just have fun!

Quiltmakers who participated in this project are: Marta Estes, *A Kaleidoscope View* (page 50); Kerry I. Hoffman, *Tasselated Cascade Majesty* (page 49); Susan I. Jones, *Pandora's Panoply* (page 49); Ursula Reikes, *Secret Garden* (page 50); Marion L. Shelton, *Hearts-A-Flower* (page 50); Barbara Weiland, *There's a Cat Loose in My Sewing Room* (page 49).

Material Girls

Seattle, Washington

This group of seven friends is part of the Block Party Quilters guild. They have been getting together for over four years and are always looking for new quilting challenges. They saw the Round Robin idea as an opportunity to work with themes, rules, colors, and techniques they might not choose on their own. The completed quilts were exhibited together at the Block Party Quilters' 1993 Quilt Show.

Progressive Quilt 1992 Rules

1. Create the original start-up block/blocks for your quilt. From there, it goes sequentially to the other members of the group, and each one adds something new to your quilt top.
2. Include a piece of muslin for the others to document their work on your quilt. This can be incorporated into the back of the quilt.
3. The monthly schedule lists the completed work you need to bring to the meeting.

May: Bring your block or blocks to pass to the next quilter. The center shape can be a square or a rectangle. Let the dimensions land somewhere between 18" and 24". Bring your muslin for others to sign as the quilt progresses.

June: Add borders no wider than 6" each to *only two sides* of the center block. Incorporate triangles into the borders.

July: Add borders to the remaining two sides, incorporating a Four-Patch or a Ninepatch design. You can add one of these or multiples. Borders must not exceed 6" in width.

August: Add borders no wider than 3" to two sides only, incorporating a solid-colored fabric.

September: Add borders no wider than 3" to the remaining two sides, incorporating a gradation of colors in several fabrics or five shades of a single color.

October: Appliqué anywhere on the project.

November: Add a final border, no wider than 5", to pull everything together, incorporating four or more of the following: growing things, stars, checkerboards, creatures with two legs, fans, curves, bow ties, photo transfer, paisley, stripes, polka dots, and wallpaper stripes.

Quiltmakers who participated in this project are pictured in a group photo below. Gillian Smith was also a member of this group. She has moved to Illinois and was not present for the photography session. Christine A. Davis, *Hawaiian Helladay*; Lori A. Fleisher, *As Above So Below*; Janine Boileau Lauderback, *Mick in the Moon*; Juliann Phillips, *Little Cabin in the Woods*; Barbie Pratt, *Tin Men, Seven Women*; Cynthia Stroo, *Living in a Material World* (page 22, label pictured on page 98).

Palouse Patchers
Moscow, Idaho

"What turned out as a modest proposal to my quilt group turned into an enormous success. Expecting a mere 10—15 people to participate in this project, we were surprised when 42 quilters signed up."
Terry Johnson-Huhta

This group of quilters had a terrific response to a request for participants interested in a Round Robin project. The goal was for each participant to create an individualized quilt with the help of five friends who added progressive borders to a center block.

These Border Beauties Round Robin quilts were made by the Material Girls, who live in the Seattle, Washington area. They have a unique, asymmetrical appearance because each member added only two borders to each quilt. (Christine A. Davis, Lori A. Fleisher, Janine Boileau Lauderback, Juliann Phillips, Barbie Pratt, Cynthia Stroo.)

Names were drawn from a hat to organize the participants into small groups, and projects were exchanged in October 1991. At the final rotation in May 1992, the group had a mini quilt show held in conjunction with their annual potluck dinner. Many of these quilts were completed and displayed at the Palouse Patchers 1993 Quilt Show.

Merry-Go-Round Medallion Rules

1. Make a block in the fabrics and design of your choice. The block should be 12"–18" square.
2. Send the block to the next person on the list, who will add the first border. Continue until each of the friends on the list have added a border. Each person will sew a total of five different borders, each one for a different block.
3. Once you sign up for the exchange, you are committed to meeting the deadlines and finishing the project. Other people are depending on you.
4. Send along 1 yard of fabric with your block so that participants can use it to provide some design continuity. Trust your friends to use just the right design and additional fabrics. You will not see your block again until May.
5. Do your best work. Respect the projects.
6. Always measure, measure, measure to make sure you are adding "square" borders to the quilt. If you are unsure of how to do this or have any other questions, check with the resource people. We could even have a mini-class before or after the meeting.

Rotation Schedule

The rotation dates, group members, and order of rotation are listed below.

1. First meeting: Sign up to participate. Make a completed center block and bring to the next meeting. We will have a list of your group ready for you. You will always pass the growing block you have just completed to the person following your name on the rotation list. The person at the bottom of the list passes to the person at the top.
2. Round 1: Add a border made of triangles.
3. Round 2: Add an appliquéd border. You have two months to do this because of the size of the project by now and the time it takes to appliqué.
4. Round 3: Add a border made of squares, rectangles, or a combination of the two.
5. Round 4: Curved border
6. Round 5: Geometric or anything-goes border

Happy Quilting!

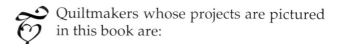 Quiltmakers whose projects are pictured in this book are:

Lorna Flack Druffel, *Gracious Generosity* (page 21, label pictured on page 99), Judy Ferguson, MayBelle Carson, Pat Hungerford, Marianne Shup, and Arlene Jonas

Terry Johnson-Huhta, *Full Circle* (page 51), Lois Roberts, Sara Jane Perino, Emma Johann, Joan Cass, and Christine Flack Schultz

Sara Jane Perino, *Gee, What a Great Group!!* (page 54), Emma Johann, Joan Cass, Christine Flack Schultz, Terry Johnson-Huhta, and Lois Roberts

Christine Flack Schultz, *Tulip Medallion* (page 47), Terry Johnson-Huhta, Lois Roberts, Sara Jane Perino, Emma Johann, and Joan Cass

Barbara B. Stellmon, *Courtyard of Roses* (page 54), Pat Maixner Magaret, Sharon Heslop Wiser, Beverly Yates, Donna Ingram Slusser, and Jan Peterson

Suggested Block Patterns

Following are the cutting and piecing directions for seven blocks that are appropriate for the center medallion in Border Beauties projects. Of course, you are free to use any other design of your choice.

Sunflower House
Sara Jane Perino

Sunflower House

Block size: 12"

Materials: Assorted fabrics from the owner's color scheme for the project

Cutting and Assembly

1. Using the templates on pages 116–17 and the pullout pattern insert, cut the required number of pieces from the desired fabrics.

2. Following the piecing diagram opposite, assemble each row. Sew rows 1 and 2 together. Sew rows 3, 4, and 5 together, adding #9 to each side last. Sew the two resulting units together.

3. Optional: Embroider or use a permanent marking tool to make lines in the windows.

4. Optional: Sewing 1½"-wide strips of background fabric to all four sides of the block adds a nice frame. Sew strips to the sides of the house first, then to the top and bottom edges. The finished size of the block with borders will be 14" x 14".

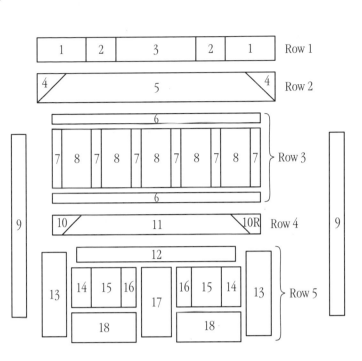

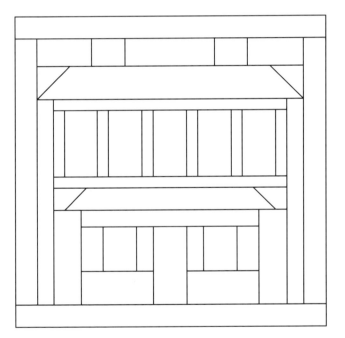

Border Suggestions:

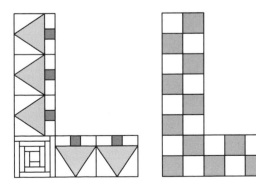

Royal Holiday
Pat Magaret

Royal Holiday

Block Size: 12"

Materials: Assorted fabrics from the owner's color scheme for the project

Cutting and Assembly

1. Using the templates on page 118, cut the required number of pieces from the desired fabrics.
2. To assist in matching the pieces accurately for machine stitching, mark the seam intersections *on the wrong side of each piece.* Use a mechanical pencil to mark cross hairs at each intersection.

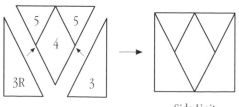

3. Make 4 side units as shown.

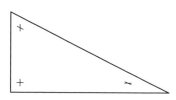

Side Unit
Make 4.

4. Make 4 corner units as shown.

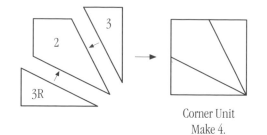

Corner Unit
Make 4.

5. Make 4 outer corner units as shown.

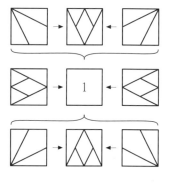

Outer Corner Unit
Make 4.

6. Arrange the side and corner units, plus piece #1, in 3 rows as shown. Sew the units together in rows. Then sew the rows together.

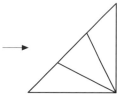

7. Add the outer corner units last.

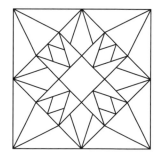

Border Suggestions:

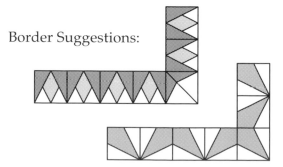

Star Dust
Donna Slusser

Star Dust

Block Size: 12"

Materials: Assorted fabrics from the owner's color scheme for the project

Cutting and Assembly

1. Using the templates on page 119, cut the required number of pieces from the desired fabrics.
2. To assist in matching the pieces accurately for machine stitching, mark the seam intersections on the wrong side of each piece. Use a mechanical pencil to mark cross hairs at each one.

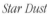

3. To make the center unit, stitch each piece #1 to a piece #2, ending the stitching ¼" from the inner point as shown. Backstitch carefully. Press all seams clockwise.

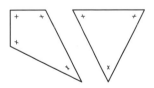

Make 4.

Sew the pairs together to make 2 halves of the center unit. Press all seams clockwise.

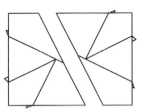

Join the 2 halves as shown.

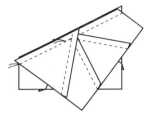

4. Make 4 corner units. Make 2 of Unit A and 2 of Unit B as shown.

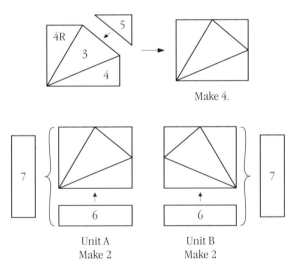

Unit A
Make 2

Unit B
Make 2

5. Make 4 side units as shown.

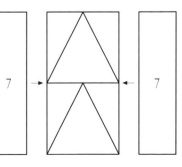

6. Arrange the completed units in rows as shown. Sew the units together in rows, then sew the rows together to complete the block.

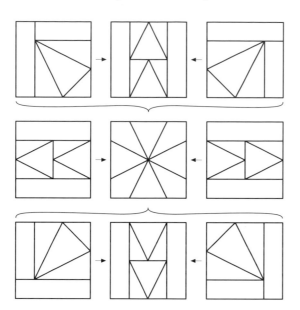

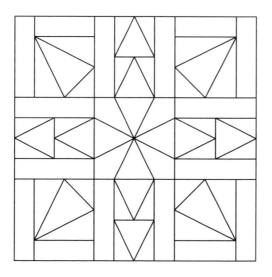

Border Suggestions:

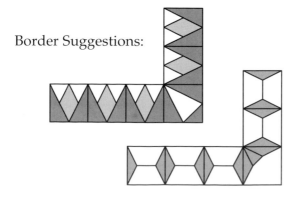

Star Frame
Donna Slusser

Star Frame

Block Size: 12"

Materials: Assorted fabrics from the owner's color scheme for the project. If you wish, you can use a fabric with a special motif in the center square.

Cutting and Assembly

1. Using the templates on page 123, cut the required number of pieces from the desired fabrics.

2. To assist in matching the pieces accurately for machine stitching, mark the seam intersections on the wrong side of each piece. Use a mechanical pencil to mark cross hairs at each intersection.

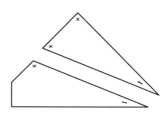

3. Sew each piece #3 to a piece #4 and each piece #3r to a piece #4r. Press seams toward the darker of the two pieces in each pair. Sew the pairs together to make 4 corner units.

4. Add piece #2 to each corner unit. Press the seam toward piece #2.

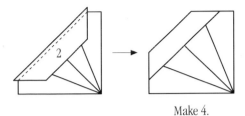

Make 4.

5. Sew each corner unit to piece #1, beginning and ending the stitching ¼" from each end of the seam. Backstitch carefully.

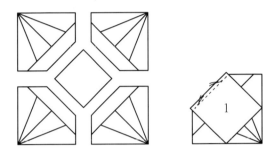

6. Fold the resulting unfinished square in half with right sides together and sew the remaining seams. Begin stitching at the outer edge of the block and sew toward the center square. Stop at the point where the previous stitching ended.

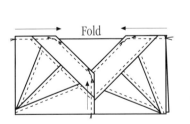

Fold

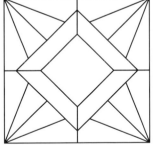

Border Suggestions:

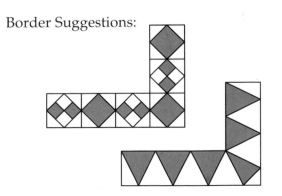

Basket of Tulips
Chris Schultz

Basket of Tulips

Block Size: 12"

Materials: Assorted fabrics from the owner's color scheme for the project

Cutting and Assembly

1. Use the templates on the pullout pattern insert. Referring to the directions on page 104, make templates for each flower and leaf and cut the required pieces from the desired fabrics.

2. Make an 18"-long piece of ⅜"-wide bias for the handle and a 12"-long piece of ¼"-wide bias for the stems. Follow the directions on page 105.

3. To make the basket, assemble 4 rows, each containing 7 squares (piece #3). Press the seams in opposite directions, row to row. Join the rows, then add piece #2 to each side and piece #1 to the bottom edge. Press seams toward the large triangles.

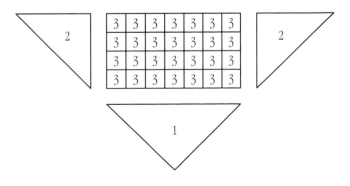

4. Appliqué all leaves, flowers, and stems (except piece #11) in place on piece #4. Refer to the basic appliqué directions on pages 103–5.
5. Sew the completed appliqué unit to the basket unit.

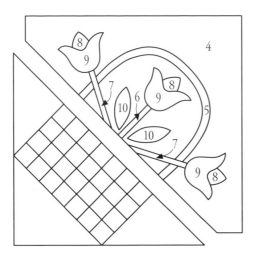

6. Appliqué piece #11 to the block.

Border Suggestions:

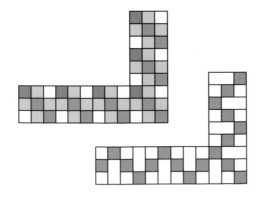

Celestial Wreath
Pat Magaret

Celestial Wreath

Block Size: 12"
Materials: Assorted fabrics from the owner's color scheme for the project

Cutting and Assembly

1. Using the templates on page 121, cut the required number of pieces from the desired fabrics. Using the leaf template on page 120 and referring to the directions on pages 103–5, cut the required number of leaves.
2. To assist in matching the star pieces accurately for machine stitching, mark the seam intersections on the wrong side of each piece. Use a mechanical pencil to mark cross hairs at each intersection.

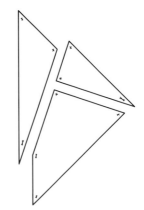

3. Prepare 1¼ yards of ³⁄₁₆"-wide bias for the stems, following the directions on page 105. This can be made in several pieces.

4. Sew each piece #3 to a piece #2. Baste a 10" length of the bias stem to piece #2 as shown, then add piece #4 to each unit.

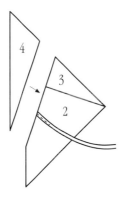

5. Repeat step 4 with pieces #2 reversed, #3 reversed, and #4 reversed, but *do not add a bias stem to the resulting units.*

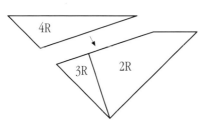

6. Sew each Unit 2/3/4 to a Unit 2r/3r/4r.

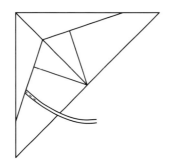

7. Add a piece #1 to the long edge of each unit, being careful not to catch the loose bias strip in the seam.

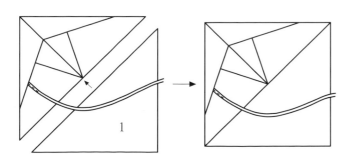

8. Sew completed units together in pairs as shown, then sew the pairs together to complete the block.

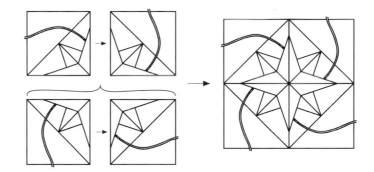

9. Appliqué the stems and leaves to the block, following the placement lines on the pattern (page 120). Refer to directions on pages 104–5.

Border Suggestions:

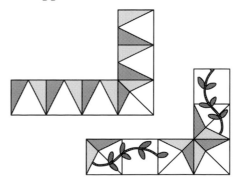

Tangled Rhodies
Pat Magaret

Tangled Rhodies

Block Size: 12"

Materials: Assorted fabrics from the owner's color scheme for the project, plus a 12½" x 12½" background square

Cutting and Assembly

1. Using the templates on the pullout pattern insert and referring to the directions on page 104, cut the required number of leaves and hearts from the desired fabrics.
2. Prepare 2¾ yards of ¼"-wide bias for stems, following the directions on page 105. This can be in several pieces.
3. *Optional*: To create the effect in the photo, a coordinating fabric was added inside the bias-stem loops. If you wish to do this, cut the pieces and baste in place on the background block before positioning and stitching the stems in place so they cover the raw edges of the added pieces.
4. Appliqué bias stems in place, referring to the basic appliqué directions on pages 103–5. See the illustration below for the placement of the continuous stem to achieve the "over-under" effect. Appliqué both sides of the stem. Leave openings where necessary to place the stem in the "under" position. Always start and end the stem where it is in the "under" position and the raw edges are covered.

5. Appliqué the leaves and hearts in place, referring to the basis appliqué directions on pages 103–5.

Border Suggestions:

Gallery of Border Beauties

Old-Fashioned Star (above) by Rachel A. Nichols, 1993, Lacey, Washington, 69" x 69". The lovely Feathered Star in the center is highlighted by colors used in the borders. (Owned by Sara Rea.)

Tulip Medallion (right) by Christine Flack Schultz, 1993, Moscow, Idaho, 55" x 55". The appliqué tulip border echoes the tulip theme.

Black and White and Red All Over (above) by Dotti Wilke, 1993, Lacey, Washington, 53" x 53". Floral motifs are framed by an outer border that gives the illusion of curves. Lily shapes are repeated in the outer corners.

Magenta Magic (right) by Sara L. Quattlebaum, 1993, Redstone Arsenal, Alabama, 60" x 60". The two outer borders were coordinated to give the appearance of one large border, resulting in this lovely effect.

Tasselated Cascade Majesty by Kerry I. Hoffman, 1994, Mercer Island, Washington, 57½" x 66½". Kerry's friends blended fabrics and shapes to give the flavor of an Oriental rug to this quilt.

Pandora's Panoply by Susan I. Jones, 1994, Bellevue, Washington, 63" x 64". Susan's friends used nicely integrated colors and shapes to give a beautiful unified look to this quilt.

There's a Cat Loose in My Sewing Room by Barbara Weiland, 1994, Redmond, Washington, 53½" x 59". Some of Barbara's favorite things are scattered throughout this colorful quilt.

A Kaleidoscope View by Marta Estes, 1994, Lake Stevens, Washington, 42" x 42". The curving lines of the Broderie Perse appliqué in the outer borders provide contrast to the straight lines of the many triangles in this quilt.

Secret Garden by Ursula Reikes, 1994, Issaquah, Washington, 60" x 69". Asymmetrical outer borders add interest and invite the viewer to walk into this quilt.

Hearts-a-Flower (right) by Marion L. Shelton, 1994, Redmond, Washington, 72" x 72". Marion's friends used some of her favorite colors to create a springtime garden quilt.

Full Circle (above) by Terry Johnson-Huhta, 1992, Moscow, Idaho, 64" x 64". Shapes in the inner border of this quilt have been enlarged and repeated in the outer border, giving unity to the design.

Bejeweled (right) by Pam Bryceson, 1993, Newman Lake, Washington, 60" x 60". The design elements and colors of the first border are coordinated beautifully with the center block in this quilt.

Voyager (above) by Thine Lu Bloxham, 1993, Hayden Lake, Idaho, 65" x 65". The Delectable Mountains outer border makes a wonderful frame for this quilt. Sewing motifs and flowers reflect Thine's interests.

I Can't Believe It's Mine! (left) by Ute M. Jarasitis, 1993, Fort Lewis, Washington, 42" x 42". The sharp points in the different borders are softened by the beautiful appliqué.

To Market to Market (above) by Ardell Powers Parkin, 1993, Coeur d'Alene, Idaho, 76" x 76". Beautiful floral appliqué softens the many points in the piecing.

Midnight Sunflower (right) by Jean VanBockel, 1993, Coeur d'Alene, Idaho, 66" x 66". Colors emphasize the theme, and Star blocks turn into sunflowers like magic.

Gee, What a Great Group!! (above) by Sara Jane Perino, 1993, Pullman, Washington, 55" x 55". Janie's friends used a lovely combination of repeated colors and theme ideas to give a crisp, beautiful look to this Border Beauties Round Robin quilt.

Courtyard of Roses (right) by Barbara Stellmon, 1993, Moscow, Idaho, 58½" x 58½". Repetition of the roses theme and gradations of value in the small squares bring continuity to this lovely quilt.

All My Quilting Friends Are Stars (above) by Gayle Noyes, 1993, Post Falls, Idaho, 74" x 74". This quilt's spectacular Friendship border is reminiscent of the landscape, character, and beauty of northern Idaho.

Add-On Appliqué

Round Robin Quilts

Friends are like a garden.
Plant seeds in good soil.
Nurture with care.
Watch it bloom.

Hattie Stava

Add-On Appliqué quilts are wall quilts based on a pictorial theme, an idea, or a subject. It is a format that is particularly fun for those who enjoy appliqué or for those who want to practice and improve their appliqué skills. It also offers a very realistic method of expression. Examine the Add-On Appliqué quilts pictured on pages 57–63 to see what we mean.

"I was a new member of our group and came to the meeting where the third rotation was taking place. Show-and-tell of these projects was unbelievable! I had to decide if I was going to participate since the group generously said I could catch up if I wanted to be a part of this project. That night I was bombarded with all these ideas that kept flashing through my mind—themes for my own quilt, visions of what I could add to all the other projects. My mind was going in circles and I didn't sleep a wink! I finally decided to become a participant, selected a Japanese theme for my project, and appliquéd bamboo on the left side of the background. I worked diligently on the other's projects and they worked speedily on mine and soon we were all caught up. I love this quilt; it is one of my favorites. What a tribute to friendship!"

Eleanor Cole

The finished quilts may look overwhelming when you are thinking in terms of a group project, but when the concept is broken down into simple steps, these quilts are much easier to make than they look. Ideas to help take the mystery out of planning the designs and adding to them begin on page 57.

The Nutcracker is an Add-On Appliqué Round Robin quilt. It begins with a background and a few appliquéd theme motifs prepared by the owner to set the stage for the story or theme.

Friends add motifs and characters that enhance the theme of the project.

The Add-On Appliqué Process

The majority of Add-On Appliqué Round Robin quilts are pictorial, so the first step is to pick a theme for the project. The owner sets the stage by providing a background in a size that falls within the group guidelines and then appliqués one or several theme motifs onto it to set the color scheme, mood, and design scale. Participants consider these elements whenever they work on the piece to provide continuity.

On the designated day, the background and other items, selected in accordance with group guidelines, are passed along in the owner's box to the next person in the predetermined rotation order. With each rotation, the quilter appliqués motif(s) that help interpret and enhance the original theme. When all rotations have been completed, the quilt is returned to its owner.

The Nutcracker, pictured in progress on page 56, is shown as it appeared at the beginning of its Round Robin journey. A window, curtains, and other basic motifs were appliquéd to a pieced background. As the quilt top progressed through its rotations, participants added characters and motifs to bring the story of the Nutcracker to life. The beautiful result is pictured below.

Add-On Appliqué Guidelines

Discuss the following criteria to set the project guidelines. After agreeing on guidelines, type, copy, and distribute them to all participants. In addition to the guidelines, be sure to include the participants' names, addresses, and telephone numbers, and the order and dates of the rotations.

Group Size

This project can accommodate a large number of quilters. A group of eight to twelve persons is good if the quilts can be rotated every two to four weeks. A minimum of eight quilters is needed to make a significant addition to any theme, unless fewer people are willing to make more motifs. The larger the number of participants, the fewer motifs each must add to the project. The larger the group, the longer the time required to complete the rotations.

Project Size and Background

Establish the size of the background. Remember that most owners will add a border or two to the quilt top after the rotations are completed and it is back in their hands. The group may agree on an exact size for the background, such as 30" x 30". Some groups might prefer a range, such as

The Nutcracker by Pat Maixner Magaret, Donna Ingram Slusser, and friends, 1994, Pullman, Washington, 55" x 35". The makers of this holiday-time theme quilt enjoyed adding characters to make the scene come to life. Children's storybooks were inspiration for the characters.

between 28" x 28" and 32" x 32". Other groups may have a guideline that states the shape of the background is optional as long as it conforms to the approximate overall size. For example, if "the background is to be 24" x 24" or equivalent," a rectangle that is 20" x 28" falls within the guidelines. If a rectangular shape is desired, 20" x 28" works nicely. This shape can be oriented either horizontally or vertically.

The background can be a single piece of fabric, or it can be created with piecing or appliqué. It should be a little larger than the desired finished size to allow for seam allowances and fabric take-up during the appliqué process. Specific information on backgrounds begins on page 60.

Adding Motifs

Part of the charm of Add-On Appliqué Round Robin quilts is working with other quilter's themes and subjects. Be prepared to do some research for each project. It is fun to read background information and gather ideas for motifs that will become an integral part of the design.

It is difficult to state the actual number of motifs each member can add to a project. Sometimes only one motif is necessary to carry out an idea. One person added Mt. Fuji to Oriental Memories, below. Other times, a participant may add motifs in several areas of the design. For example, in Amish Summer, page 59, one participant added a barn and an Amish farmer holding a pig. Decide if you can overlap new additions or place them under previously completed motifs.

Appliqué Techniques

Indicate whether appliqué additions are to be done by hand or machine or whether either method can be used.

Embellishments

Decide whether embellishments are OK. Consider embroidery, inking, beads, buttons, ribbons, and lace, for example.

Rotation Order and Time Schedule

Establish the rotation order and dates. The amount of time between exchanges depends upon the experience and time schedules of group members. Allow enough time for research, creativity, and planning as well as time to do the appliqué. Add extra time if holidays fall within a rotation. A month is usually an adequate amount of time to add several motifs to the projects. However, some groups have been known to plan rotations for every two or three weeks.

Oriental Memories by Eleanor Kiser Cole, 1993, Pullman, Washington, 32½" x 33½". Eleanor's friends created this beautiful quilt that brings back fond memories of a trip to the Orient.

Show-and-Tell

Detailed information and options are given in the section on "Guidelines for All Groups" on pages 13–15.

Items to Include in the Owner's Box

Owners can include a journal, fabrics, and other items according to group guidelines. For ideas, see pages 16–17.

Owner's Options

Decide whether the owners can make changes after the projects are returned to them. Refer to page 61 in this chapter for additional information.

Mini-Workshops

Since appliqué is the only technique used in this Round Robin project, the group might want to plan demonstrations on several types of appliqué, such as the needle-turn method or the freezer-paper method. Refer to pages 103–5 in "Basic Quiltmaking Techniques" or to any of the appliqué references listed in the "Bibliography" on page 128.

Another workshop might be spent discussing the section on "Design Basics," beginning on page 85. If there is a group member with an art background, arrange for that person to share ideas about composition, scale, value, and the other elements and principles of design.

Reunion Party

Set a tentative date for a reunion party, when the projects will be completely finished. Refer to the information on page 15.

Selecting a Project Theme

What do you like? Select a subject that reflects your interests. Your enthusiasm for the theme will be contagious and create excitement for the other participants. Thumb through books in your personal library and if necessary, take a trip to your public library. Look at art books, books on nature, and travel guides. Children's books are particularly inspirational and often portray images in a simplistic line-drawing style. These are easy to modify for appliqué motifs. Coloring books also offer good ideas. Greeting cards, wrapping paper, cookie cutters, posters, and calendars all yield an abundance of inspiration. Don't forget magazines and photographs.

Explore themes that have many ideas for motifs that you can add to support the main idea. Some theme ideas to explore include: jungle and zoo; dinosaurs; pets; underwater scenes; flower gardens; scenes that depict a way of life; scenes from foreign countries; cityscapes; farm scenes; biblical themes, such as the tree of life; vacation memories; seasonal settings; holiday motifs; pure fantasy; scenes from favorite literature, TV, and movies.

Amish Summer by Shirley Perryman, 1993, Pullman, Washington, 34" x 34". Friends had fun finding ideas and interpreting them in fabric to create this Amish countryside scene.

Selecting Color and Fabric

The Background

The background fabric is the backdrop for the subject or theme. It must enhance the subject but, at the same time, remain in the background and not compete with the theme. As you decide on the background fabrics, ask yourself the following questions.

ᘐ Do I want to create a scene that will be bright and joyful or calm and serene?

ᘐ Do I want a light, medium, or dark background? Does the time of day matter?

ᘐ What about texture? A snowy scene may require a print that reads "snow," for example.

Background fabrics are usually solid colors or small prints that give the appearance of texture but look like solids when viewed from a distance. A neutral color, such as beige, pale green, or a soft, muted blue, makes a good backdrop for a theme or story. Avoid busy background fabrics because they distract from the appliqué motifs.

When preparing the background, remember it can be whole cloth, pieced, or appliquéd. If the scene is to be a landscape, it is better to divide the background unevenly. For example, avoid making it half sky and half land mass. It is more pleasing to use a 2 : 1 ratio—two parts land to one part sky, or two parts sky to one part land. Use whichever option is best for the effect you desire.

Cut or make the background several inches larger than the predetermined finished size. It can be "sized" later, after the last motif has been added. On this oversized background, mark the exact size of the finished top to indicate that all appliqué is to be placed within this area. Always pretest the marking tool before using on the actual background fabric.

The first images on the quilt, appliquéd by the owner, often form the backdrop for other, more interesting motifs that will be added later. These first images set the size and proportion for later additions. For example, the owner appliquéd the window, drapes, and Christmas tree to the background of "The Nutcracker" (pages 56–57). Group members added the story's characters to create the focal point and secondary points of interest.

Sometimes, the focal point or area of emphasis is the first piece the owner adds to the background. Then group members add supporting motifs that carry out the theme. In "Flora, Fauna, and Friends," at left, Pat appliquéd the tree and ocean waves to her background. Other participants appliquéd various motifs that brought "life" to the design.

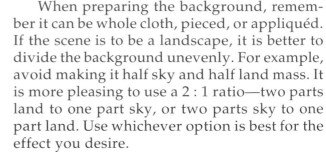

Flora, Fauna, and Friends by Pat Maixner Magaret, 1994, Pullman, Washington, 29" x 32½". This quilt began as a Tree of Life design but changed its course when the snake and apple were added. Other motifs turned it into a beautiful garden.

The Add-Ons

Refer to the general information on pages 18 and 101 to guide your fabric choices for the motifs you add to each participant's quilt top. In addition, the following suggestions may prove helpful.

🖎 Be sure to have a good balance of lights, mediums, and darks.

🖎 Use a variety of textures. Part of the fun and challenge of this project can be searching for prints with a visual texture that is the same as the real-life motif being portrayed. Look for wood-grain prints to use for tree trunks or windowsills, ripple prints for rivers and streams, and feather prints for birds' wings, for example.

🖎 Generally speaking, use small-scale prints, since most of the appliqué pieces will be rather small. However, don't overlook large-scale prints completely. Sometimes you can isolate part of a large-scale print that has just the right texture for the piece you are creating

🖎 Most of the fabrics should read as solids from a distance. When values are similar, colors and lines will run together, blending rather than defining the edges between the various appliqué pieces in the motif. When there is high contrast, edges are sharp and lines are strongly defined. Do not use too many busy prints, particularly next to each other.

🖎 Try using a fabric that is almost the same as one that has already been used in the design. This creates subtle impressions of texture and dimension. Turn the fabric over and use the back side when appropriate.

🖎 Repeat fabrics in different places on the background to create balance and give continuity to the design.

🖎 For a special splash of glitz, use lamé, satin, or polished cotton. Try corduroy or velvet to add definite tactile texture. You may have to sacrifice ease of appliqué when using these specialty fabrics to obtain the desired effect. Take extra care when handling these fabrics.

🖎 Embellishments invite the viewer to come closer to the quilt. If you plan to include embellishments, use only those that enhance the design. Don't overdo. Remember the potential use and purpose of this quilt and the extra care it will need if embellishments are added.

Treat each quilt top as if it were your own, always contributing to the unity of the design. Use appropriate motifs and colors and keep the additions in scale, proportion, and balance with the other motifs already on the background piece.

If you want to hide part of a motif behind another appliquéd piece, you may need to remove a few stitches in order to slip the raw edges of your piece underneath. Carefully replace any stitches you remove.

Finishing the Design

Some projects need little or no work to make them complete after they are returned to their owners. For example, "Oriental Memories" on page 58 needed only borders to frame the picture and complete the quilt top. Other projects will need additional work to complete the project.

Refer to the group's guidelines with regard to making changes. Are you allowed to move existing motifs or add pieces on top or underneath them? Does the design need more motifs to fill in blank spaces? Refer to the suggestions and tips in "Design Basics," beginning on page 85, to help bring unity and balance to the design if needed. For those projects that look somewhat bare, add enough shapes and motifs to make the design look harmonious and unified. When Pat's "Flora, Fauna, and Friends" quilt on page 60 was returned to her, it had a lot of blank spaces. She added all the leaves, the bird and nest, several flowers, Adam and Eve, winding ivy, and the fish to create the appearance of a lush garden setting.

In the interest of friendship, if you find it necessary to move, overlap, or change any previously placed pieces, ask or inform the person who added it to your quilt top.

When the design is finished to the owner's satisfaction, it is time to add borders and finish the quilt. Refer to pages 95–97 for further help in selecting borders and quilting designs.

Add-On Appliqué projects are a fun way to improve your skills and stretch creativity. Congratulations! You are now a Master Motif Maker, an Artistic Appliqué Architect, and a Systematic Scene Stitcher.

Sample Group Guidelines

Rock Creek Quilters
Fairfield, Washington

In the spring of 1991, twenty-six members of this group decided to make the progressive dollhouse wall quilt shown below. The rotation order was determined by drawing numbers out of a hat. As each member worked on the dollhouse, they wrote about their experience in a journal sent along with the project. In this journal, the quilters could describe why a particular item was added, discuss events in the world and their lives at the time, and include their timely thoughts about things in general. Every third person took a picture of the "house raising" with the camera provided in the project box. These photos were later added to the journal and helped make it as special as the quilt itself. This beautiful quilt was completed in six months in order to be included in the Washington State Quilters (Spokane Chapter) 1992 Quilt Show.

Progressive Dollhouse Quilt Rules

1. All methods of sewing or embroidery are allowed.
2. All types of fabric and materials can be used, as long as the item doesn't stick out too far.
3. It is OK to add to another person's work, but don't move it, remove it, or cover it up entirely.
4. Each participant can see the project only when working on it.
5. Each person will have one week to work on the quilt top. If they cannot take their turn, their name goes to the end of the list, and the quilt is given to the next name on the list.
6. Every third person is to take a picture of the quilt.

Quilters who participated in this project include: Raejean Allen, Jackie Anderson, Christina Birrenkott, Vicki Dormaier, Lori Hein, Kathy Hodl, Genieve Isaacson, Linda Johnson, Debbie Kelly, Maxine Kincaid, Michelle Lemke, Sheila MacDonald, Chris Mewhinney, Kathi Meyer, Julie Noble, Joan Oshanick, Jan Osler, Kathy Ottosen, Betsy Parry, Kathryn Parry, Tess Parry, Pam Richards, Jennifer Roberts, Vida Washburn, Ann Wenning, Kathy Wilkerson.

Dollhouse Quilt by Rock Creek Quilters, 1991, Fairfield, Washington, 47" x 47". This charming quilt has surprises in every room and corner to delight children of all ages.

Stitch 'n Study Quilt Group

Pullman, Washington

This small group of quilters is part of the Patchin' People Quilt Guild. These friends are always looking for new challenges and were intrigued with the concept of the progressive quilt. In the spring of 1991, they decided to make progressive wall quilts for each other using appliqué techniques. We belong to this group. The format the group used became known as the Add-On Appliqué type of Round Robin quilt. Nine quilters participated in the project. Birthdays of group members were listed in chronological order and this became the rotation order.

Quilters who participated in this project include: Eleanor Kiser Cole, "Oriental Memories" (page 58); Pat Maixner Magaret, "Flora, Fauna, and Friends" (page 60); Shirley Perryman, "Amish Summer" (page 59); Sharon Heslop Wiser, "Escape to Amorgas" (below right).

In addition to the quilts listed above that resulted from the first project, we collaborated on creating the background piece for The Nutcracker (pages 56–57). The following quilters participated in creating this group quilt: Judy Abdel-Monem, Kathleen H. Butts, Eleanor Kiser Cole, Lorna Flack Druffel, Rosy Marie Shields Ferner, Pat Maixner Magaret, Sara Jane Perino, Shirley Perryman, Lee Ellen Philpott, Joanie Ware Renfro, Daleah Thiessen, Donna Ingram Slusser, and Sharon Heslop Wiser.

Escape to Amorgas by Sharon Heslop Wiser, 1993, Pullman, Washington, 36" x 36". This wonderful vacation memory quilt is the result of Sharon's friends doing research about Greece while dining on gyros and baklava!

Around-the-Block
Round Robin Quilts

The fabric of life is woven with the golden threads of friendship.
Caroline Linnett

Around-the-Block quilts begin with a theme block that is surrounded by smaller blocks placed "around the block." The smaller blocks all relate to the theme, subject matter, and color scheme. These quilts combine elements of Border Beauties and Add-On Appliqué with the addition of a grid system similar to the one found in the book *One-of-a-Kind Quilts* by Judy Hopkins.

One of the fun aspects of Round Robin quiltmaking is that each participant has an active part in the design process for each person's quilt. The Around-the-Block format also provides this opportunity, but at the end of the rotations, the owner has the option of reorganizing the various blocks created by the participants.

These quilts have various design styles. Some are realistic while others are impressionistic in nature. Still others have a folk-art look, tell a story, or resemble a collage. Both piecing and appliqué techniques are used to create the components of the quilt top, offering the opportunity to practice a variety of skills. Creativity is encouraged when designing all blocks, whether they are quite simple or very elaborate. Examine the photos of some of the Around-the-Block Friendship quilts on pages 69–75 and let them inspire you and your friends to form a group to make these fun quilts.

Orient on My Mind by Eleanor Kiser Cole, 1993, Pullman, Washington, 40" x 47½". Eleanor will forever treasure this dramatic example of a collection of Far Eastern motifs and ideas.

The Around-the-Block Process

The Around-the-Block Round Robin project begins with each participant selecting a theme or subject and making a theme block. This block is then pinned or basted to a piece of needlepunch, such as Pellon® polyester fleece, that has been marked with a 4" x 4" grid. Following the group guidelines, each owner prepares a project box that includes the theme block, additional fabric, and information and theme resources.

The projects are passed around in a predetermined order of rotation. During each rotation, participants make the required number of 4" (finished) squares or combination of squares. Some of these smaller squares are special, more elaborate blocks that support the theme. They may be pieced or appliquéd. The remainder of the blocks serve as background or spacer squares. All small blocks should add to the theme but not outshine it. These smaller blocks are pinned or basted anywhere to the gridded fleece in any location the maker desires.

When the projects are returned to the owners, it is the owner's option to rearrange the blocks. After finalizing the position of the theme block

Orient on My Mind, (above left) an Around-the-Block Round Robin quilt, began with Eleanor's theme block and was placed on a traveling grid.

(Left) Friends made accent blocks to enhance the theme block.

and participants' blocks, it is often necessary for the owner to make additional blocks to complete the quilt top. Also, no matter how hard one tries to use all of the blocks in the design, sometimes there are a few squares left over. This is an opportunity for the owner to be creative and find another place to use these squares, perhaps in the border or on the back side of the quilt!

"Orient on My Mind" is an example of an Around-the-Block quilt and is shown in progress on page 65. Notice how it started with a theme block pinned to the fleece. Participants each made small blocks or block combinations that reflect the theme and colors of the design. When the quilt was returned to its owner, she rearranged the blocks, made slight modifications, and added a few more simple blocks. The beautiful result is pictured on page 64.

Around-the-Block Guidelines

After making decisions about the various aspects of the Around-the-Block project, type, copy, and distribute the guidelines to all participants. Include participants' names, addresses, phone numbers, and the order and dates of rotation.

Some basic formats for this type of project appear on pages 77–78. These suggested plans use a 4" x 4" grid (finished size). This size block blends well in the viewer's eye when the quilt is completed. The placement of the theme block in the diagrams is for illustration purposes only. The owner has the option of putting the theme block anywhere desired. These plans give suggestions for individual projects and include:

§ Number of participants in a group
§ Suggested size of the theme block
§ Number of blocks to be added by each participant
§ Grid size
§ Finished size of the project at the end of the rotations

Of course, there is always the option of designing a grid system based on a different size block if desired.

Group Size

This type of Round Robin project can accommodate any number of quilters. Specific suggestions for groups of five to twelve participants appear on pages 77–78.

Project Size

These quilts make wonderful wall quilts. Sizes for the projects on pages 77–78 do not include borders. Each plan could be easily adapted to a miniature quilt or to a full-size quilt. When using a size that is larger than the 4" grid, allow extra time for the rotations.

Theme-Block Size

Establish the theme-block size. Suggestions are given on pages 77–78. If you use the recommended grid size of 4" x 4", the theme block should have finished dimensions that are even multiples of 4", for example 16" x 20". It should cover approximately 20%–25% of the total design space allowed.

Some group guidelines state that the theme block is a certain size "or the approximate equivalent." This gives more flexibility, which some groups prefer. It means that participants have the option of taking the number of blocks used in the theme block and putting them into another arrangement, as long as the size of the theme block is close to the stated guideline. For example, if group guidelines state "the theme block is to be 4 squares by 4 squares (total = 16 squares) or the approximate equivalent," a rectangular block that is 3 blocks x 5 blocks (total = 15 blocks) is allowed. If the equivalent

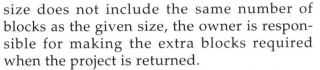

size does not include the same number of blocks as the given size, the owner is responsible for making the extra blocks required when the project is returned.

The owner may pin or baste the theme block anywhere on the gridded fleece. Suggested placement for theme blocks appears in the format grids on pages 77–78. Once positioned, the owner's theme block remains in the same place during the entire rotation process.

Supporting Blocks

These are the smaller blocks made by participants during the various rotations. They are usually based on a 4" square (finished). Group guidelines should include:

- ⑤ Number of squares to be made by each participant. In the plans given on pages 77–78, each participant makes six supporting blocks or combinations of blocks that cover a total of six squares.
- ⑤ Number of elaborate blocks and number of spacer blocks. We recommend each person make only two special blocks and four simpler blocks to be used as spacers. See pages 70–74 for additional information.

In addition, you can make larger blocks to create an area of the required size for a particular motif or theme. For example, to make the stalk and ear of corn in the McSlusser's Garden quilt on page 74, it was necessary to sew two blocks together to make the background for the appliqué.

- ⑤ Block techniques. Both appliqué and pieced blocks are appropriate for Around-the-Block quilts. When determining the guidelines, decide whether appliqué should be done by hand or machine or whether participants can use the method of their choice.
- ⑤ Block placement. Blocks previously placed on the grid cannot be moved. Participants must work within the framework created by the evolving design.
- ⑤ Block size. Blocks must be the correct size. If a 4" grid is used, blocks must measure 4½" x 4½" (unfinished size) when they are placed on the grid, where they will overlap each other slightly. It's a good idea to add a guideline stating that the owner may choose

to include or discard completed blocks that are inaccurate or distorted.

- ⑤ Signatures. Should each participant sign or initial each block they make? Some groups ask that the signatures or initials be hidden in each block. Use a permanent marking pen, such as the Pigma pen, to mark on fabric.

Embellishments

Decide whether or not participants can add embellishments, such as embroidery, inking, buttons, charms, lace, or beads, to a project. Refer to the "Guidelines for All Groups" on pages 13–15.

Rotation Order and Time Schedule

Determine the rotation order and dates that the projects will be exchanged. Keep the schedules of all participants in mind and add extra time for holidays. Allow time for research and for designing motifs and squares. You don't want participants to feel rushed. Keeping everyone happy is an essential ingredient to a successful project.

Items to Include in the Owner's Box

Place the theme block and the grid in a special traveling box along with other items listed in the guidelines. Additional information about what to include in this box appears on pages 16–17.

Show-and-Tell

Does the group want to have show-and-tell at each meeting or keep the projects a secret? See pages 14–15 for additional information.

Owner's Options

After the final rotation, the owner should have the option of adding more blocks as well as rearranging the blocks or enlarging the project if desired. During the rotations, the participants sometimes get carried away and make many elaborate blocks and not enough simple blocks. This is not bad; it simply creates another challenge for the owner.

What about blocks that just won't fit into the final design, no matter how hard the owner tries? What about putting them on the back side of the quilt or incorporating them into the label? Participants should keep an open mind about where their blocks might be placed in the final scheme of things—whether on the front or back.

Be sure to make this guideline very clear at the beginning of the project. It helps alleviate the pressure to make perfect, coordinated blocks. The Stitch 'n Study group allowed owners the option of rearranging and adding blocks as well as the option of placing a few of the blocks on the back side if necessary. See page 16 for additional information on "Owner's Options."

Mini-Workshops

Both piecing and appliqué techniques can be used in Around-the-Block quilts. The group might want to plan demonstrations on precision piecing as well as explore different methods of appliqué. The "Bibliography" on page 128 includes several books with information on these techniques.

Reunion Party

Set a tentative date for a time when the projects will be completely finished.

Using a Design Wall

When designing an Around-the-Block quilt, you'll find it's much easier to see the design develop if you place it on a vertical plane (the wall) rather than on a horizontal plane (tabletop or floor). With this type of Round Robin project, you also need to have a design surface that you can roll or fold so you can place it in the traveling box for the rotations.

Use white needlepunch fleece, such as Pellon®, for the design wall. Refer to format grids on pages 77–78 to find the size of the working wall that corresponds to the format of your project. Mark the needlepunch with a 4" x 4" grid, using a permanent marking pen. Always pretest the marking tool before using it.

If the group has ten participants, you will need a design wall that is 36" x 40". Mark a 4" x 4" grid over the surface that is 8 squares by 9 squares. It is also a good idea to write your name and phone number at the top of the grid and to mark the top edge for easy identification. The fleece acts as a flannel board, and when fabrics are pressed against it, they usually stick to it. However, when you add completed blocks to the fleece, pin or baste them so they do not become lost or misplaced during the rotation process.

Project Themes and Theme Blocks

Selecting a theme or subject matter for your project is a process that cannot be hurried. *Allow time for thinking and planning.* Look at nature and nature books, art books, greeting cards, wrapping paper, photographs, children's books, and other pictorial resources. Gather many ideas first and then make a final selection.

Use the theme block to set the mood and color scheme for the entire project. It will probably be the focal point or center of attention. Use it to introduce the subject matter, colors, and fabrics that will be used throughout the quilt. Select a theme that has numerous supporting ideas. An example might be a pieced sewing machine for a theme block with other sewing equipment and motifs as supporting blocks. "All Aboard" started with an appliquéd Noah and ark. Other members of the group added supporting blocks portraying pairs of animals.

Memorializing a family trip to Hawaii was the theme for "Around the Island" on page 75. The Hawaiian theme block was started in a quilt class while on this vacation, and participants made a variety of supporting blocks to carry out the idea.

Donna enjoys gardening, so it was natural for her to adapt her theme block for "McSlusser's Garden" (page 74) from a Beatrix Potter book. Friends had a hard time deciding which motifs to make for her since there are so many crops and gardening paraphernalia in a vegetable garden.

All Aboard by Shirley Perryman, 1994, Pullman, Washington, 51" x 42". Plaids and stripes were a natural for depicting this folk-art rendition of the familiar Bible story.

Passion for Paisley by Kathleen H. Butts, 1993, Pullman, Washington, 47" x 55½". Kathleen's appreciation for these unique prints inspired her friends to make motifs reminiscent of an Oriental rug.

The theme block can be simple or complicated. It can be pieced or appliquéd, or you can combine both techniques. Themes can be interpreted in a variety of ways: traditional, contemporary, realistic, or abstract. In "Passion for Paisley," a Drunkard's Path variation made of paisley prints inspired participants to make additional traditional blocks. A medallion with the sophisticated mood of an Oriental rug was the result.

"Living or Survival" on page 73 is a collage that depicts how we view our environment today, with both good and bad representations. It also addresses our concerns and hopes for tomorrow.

"Starry Starry Night" on page 70 started with a Crazy quilt theme block made from many solar and celestial prints. The introductory statement in the owner's journal alluded to the song "Starry Starry Night," about the life of Vincent Van Gogh. The quilt evolved into a fabric interpretation of Van Gogh's painting of the same name.

Some themes suggest a scene or landscape. Pat's "Go Tell It on the Mountain" on page 73 is an example. The theme block was the crèche scene. Friends made supporting blocks that included Bethlehem, shepherds, wise men, mountains, and other related motifs.

In addition to theme ideas already mentioned, some other suggestions include: traditional blocks that suggest smaller versions, such as stars; scenes or landscapes; holidays; favorite hobbies; vacation memories; images or symbols from other cultures; art; favorite fabrics; the seasons; nature; themes from literature, the movies, or TV; special celebrations; or favorite subjects.

Supporting Blocks

These are the smaller blocks that support the theme or serve as spacer or background blocks. Give careful thought to each addition in order to enhance the growing design. It is important to concentrate on giving the quilt top what it needs, not on making the most beautiful block in the project. Make sure that the small blocks you contribute do not take over the quilt. Also, be sure to allow yourself enough time to make the blocks, rather than rushing to start and finish them the day before the next scheduled rotation! Allow time for thinking and planning and executing the designs.

There are two types of supporting blocks: accent blocks and spacer blocks.

Accent Blocks

These are the small blocks that elaborate on the theme or subject established by the block owner. They are secondary focal points that have less attention value than the center of interest.

They bring continuity to the quilt's design and help provide balance and rhythm. They are a little more special than the spacer blocks and relate directly to the theme. They should not, however, take over the quilt. They are more labor intensive than spacer blocks and can be pieced or appliquéd, or you can combine these techniques. Other techniques may also be used if allowed in the group guidelines.

General Rules for Accent Blocks

1. Rules are made to be broken!
2. Make blocks that enrich rather than overpower the idea of the central theme. Perhaps you can add a pieced or appliqué block with a name that relates to the theme. For example, the Bear Paw pattern was used to make accent blocks for "Polar Bear Alert" on page 72. Several Chinese Puzzle blocks were made for "Orient on My Mind" on page 64, and the small versions of Hawaiian quilt motifs in "Around the Island" (page 75) are good examples of appliquéd accent blocks that support the theme.
3. Make the accent blocks "special." These blocks generally take a little more time and effort. Use appliqué or make special pieced blocks to interpret the theme and create secondary areas of emphasis. The owner of the quilt usually includes information and resources about the theme in the traveling box. Use these for inspiration. Always feel free to do more research on your own to find a motif that is "just right."

Starry Starry Night by Judy Hopkins, 1993, San Diego, California, 37" x 45". This quilt feels like a galaxy of stars. It's aptly titled after a Van Gogh painting and a song.

4. Make only one or two accent blocks for each project. Too many elaborate blocks result in a finished quilt top that is too busy. However, it is sometimes difficult to use only two squares for accent blocks when working on some themes. Go ahead and have fun making the accent blocks of your choice, even if you do end up with more than two. The owner can always add more spacer blocks after the rotations are completed if necessary.

5. The suggested block size is 4" x 4" (finished) as shown in the format grid on pages 77–78. Occasionally, a larger space is needed for a specific design or idea. Combine several of the blocks, but always stay within the grid system. For example, two squares on the grid can be combined to make a 4" x 8" rectangle; three combined make a 4" x 12" rectangle; and four blocks combined make an 8" x 8" square.

In "Dutch Winds Stir My Soul," one participant added the Amsterdam street-scene block, which covers four squares. In addition, this person made two simple spacer blocks to complete the required total of six blocks.

Be careful when using larger motifs or designs; they can overpower the main theme block if you are not careful to integrate the new block(s) with the existing composition. In the example mentioned in the previous paragraph, the Amsterdam street scene fits in nicely with the rest of the design, even though it is a larger-than-average block. It works because the fabrics and colors selected provide continuity with the others in the quilt.

6. Repeat colors and fabrics already used in other areas of the quilt top. This adds balance and continuity to the design. Sometimes there is a tendency to go wild and use something exotic. Plan carefully so that newly introduced fabrics and colors are compatible with the existing flavor of the quilt.

7. You can repeat blocks. When someone has a good idea, copy it! This also adds continuity, balance, and rhythm to the design. In "Polar Bear Alert," on page 72, one participant made a Bear Paw unit. Other participants added more Bear Paw units. Then the owner arranged these blocks in a manner that suggests a bear walking across the quilt.

8. Add to another person's idea. In "Dutch Winds Stir My Soul," below, one participant made an accent block portraying a stork and its nest on a chimney. Another quilter added a house accent block and placed it under the stork block. Such additions unify the total effect of the quilt. They are also fun to plan and design!

Spacer Blocks

Spacer blocks are just as important as the theme block and the accent blocks. Don't skimp on these simple units that play a subordinate role in the overall design. They serve as resting places for the viewer's eye and provide spaces between the theme block and various accent blocks. They also create

Dutch Winds Stir My Soul by Lee Ellen Philpott, 1993, Pullman, Washington, 38" x 46". Lee's family enjoyed watching the evolution of this quilt, a tribute to her Dutch heritage.

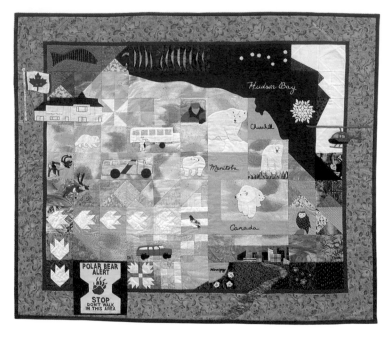

Polar Bear Alert by Jeanie Ware Renfro, 1993, Pullman, Washington, 53" x 45½". Polar bears, a train station, and a husband in an orange jacket are just a few of the highlights of a trip to Churchill, Manitoba, Canada, stitched into this quilt by friends.

Games People Play by Sharon Heslop Wiser, 1993, Pullman, Washington, 50" x 38". Sharon's family loves to play games and this quilt evokes fond memories.

background texture. Use only two or three block patterns as spacer blocks in one project; repeat them throughout the quilt. Using only a few block designs helps keep the background from becoming too busy. Format grids on pages 77–78 show examples of spacer blocks.

> ### ✑ *Tip*
>
> We all want to make beautiful and unique blocks for each of our friends' quilts. We want everything to be very special. In this type of Round Robin project, sometimes the nicest thing you can do is to repeat spacer blocks to provide a background for the beautiful accent blocks. Just remember, every star needs a good supporting cast!

General Rules for Spacer Blocks

1. Rules are made to be broken!
2. Use simple designs. Choose blocks with simple lines made of simple shapes. Look for block patterns with no more than six pieces. For examples of spacer blocks, see the chart on page 78. Templates begin on page 124.
3. Use only two to four different block patterns for the spacer blocks throughout the quilt, then repeat them. For best results, use only a few spacer block designs in a project. Repeat these designs and vary the fabric color choices. Using too many designs creates a busy look, and the different blocks fight for attention. Some of the most pleasing backgrounds contain only three or four simple blocks that have been duplicated by more than one person. In "Games People Play," the simple Four Patch was used repeatedly as a spacer block.

    Not only does this give continuity to the design, it also suggests a checkerboard, a nice reinforcement of the theme.
4. Make at least two or three spacer blocks for every accent block you make.
5. Use neutral or subdued fabrics. These blocks play an important role. Select fabrics that suggest texture and interest without dominating.
6. Repeat fabrics. This adds continuity to the overall design. Try using similar fabrics or use the back side of a print that has already been used in the quilt top for subtle contrast and texture.
7. Use only block designs based on a four-patch format, particularly when using the 4" x 4" grid

and making 4" (finished) blocks. It makes the mathematics easy to figure when cutting and sewing. The math is more difficult if you use block designs based on nine-patch or five-patch formats. In addition, the seams will not match other blocks.

Using the same basic block format gives the background a common, unified visual look. The lines of these similar units flow with ease across the quilt because the seams of each block match the seams of the neighboring blocks. The blocks on page 78 are based on the four-patch format. Other examples can be found in many quilting books that contain traditional and original designs. These books often list the blocks under a four-patch category. See the "Bibliography" on page 128.

8. Spacer blocks can be pointers, leading the eye to different areas of the design. In "Orient on My Mind" on page 64, the red in the spacer blocks produces a flow throughout the quilt as well as a frame for the theme block. Repetition of half-square triangles and variations of the simple block produce diagonal lines streaming across the design. In "Go Tell It on the Mountain," below right, the use of these units gives the illusion that light is radiating from the stable. The same unit can be repeated and arranged to give the feel of mountains.

Consider common patchwork units that can be used in several ways. For example, you can use the Flying Geese unit to represent trees as well as birds. The Square-in-a-Square unit gives a peephole or Swiss-cheese look to a quilt. You can place motifs in the center of these units as was done in "Living or Survival," where faces from our crowded earth peek out at us from the center of the blocks.

Living or Survival (above right) by Rose Marie Shields Ferner, 1993, Moscow, Idaho, 52" x 60". A collage portrays hopes and concerns for the future of our environment.

Go Tell It on the Mountain (right) by Patricia Maixner Magaret, 1993, Pullman, Washington, 42" x 54". Pat always wanted a nativity-scene quilt. Thanks to her friends, she now has one she can enjoy every Christmas.

9. Generally speaking, you will need more spacer blocks near the end of the project. As the Around-the-Block projects are passed along, the main areas on the grid fill up with completed accent and spacer blocks. By the time the last two people on the rotation schedule receive the project, there are mostly single spaces waiting to be filled and the designs can be rather busy. Spacer blocks, rather than accent blocks, are needed.

Sometimes a participant might want to make an accent block that requires a multi-block format and there is no room on the grid. Check with the owner of the quilt top for approval to place it outside the outer edges of the predetermined grid lines. For example, one participant wanted to make the four-space "sun block" for the "McSlusser's Garden" quilt, below right, when there were only single spaces remaining on the grid. Donna gave her permission to place the completed design in the upper left-hand corner of the quilt design, extending it beyond the grid into the border, where it remains today!

Finishing the Design

After the design wall has made all of its scheduled stops, it returns to its original owner. Usually, there is more work to do, but before you start to finish your quilt top, refer to the group's guidelines about making changes. If you are having difficulty creating unity with the blocks, refer to "Design Basics" on pages 85–94 for ideas you can use to make your design more cohesive.

Depending on the group guidelines, consider the following possibilities as you assemble the wonderful blocks that you have received.

Rearranging the Design

All the owners of the Around-the-Block quilts pictured in this book rearranged their blocks after the projects were returned to them. Some projects required minimal change. Others required major adjustments to create a pleasing design, including moving the theme block. This is not bad or good. It is part of the challenge for the owner!

A good example of this adjustment is illustrated in "Orient on My Mind" on page 64. Notice how the design looked during the rotations (page 65) and how it looks in the

completed quilt. Eleanor moved the red in the spacer blocks to produce a flow throughout the quilt as well as to frame the theme block.

Adding Blocks

After rearranging the design, you may need to add blocks. When "McSlusser's Garden" was returned to Donna, the accent blocks covered over forty spaces on the grid and there were only twenty-two spacer blocks in the design! Her friends had so much fun making the unique garden accent blocks that they forgot to make enough spacer blocks. Donna's challenge was to bring order out of the busy chaos. First, she moved the largest accent blocks out beyond the corners of the grid and added one additional row of blocks to the top and another row to the left side of the project.

Next, she moved the remaining accent blocks to create garden rows and interest areas that act as secondary focal points, such as the scarecrow, the bunny at the garden gate, and the wheelbarrow. Then she made twenty-two additional spacer blocks and used them to create the necessary

McSlusser's Garden by Donna Ingram Slusser, 1994, Pullman, Washington, 36" x 44". Donna loves to garden. Her friends made sure she can enjoy her passion all year 'round.

background between the rows as well as the garden path that helps take the eye around the design. These changes had the effect of quieting a rather busy design and bringing unity to the composition.

Moving Blocks to the Back

Sometimes a block seems appropriate when it is first made and added to the growing quilt top, but in the end, no matter how hard the owner tries to include it, it just won't fit into the overall scheme of things. When this happens, don't give up too soon. Solving the problem is an opportunity to exercise creativity, but when all your efforts fail, consider using the block or blocks in the borders or on the back of the quilt. Perhaps you can use one or more of them to create an interesting label.

If you move blocks, we suggest that you have a one-on-one chat with the block maker(s) before the unveiling of the finished quilt to let them know where their blocks have been placed. That way, they won't be disappointed when they see the quilt the first time and discover their blocks missing from the front.

Making Minor Changes

To create a finished quilt design that has unity, you may need to change someone's block. Again, ask permission from the person or notify them of your plans. The design of "Around the Island," below, was improved by changing one of the pieces in the Pinwheel blocks around the center theme. The block maker did not object and the result is a more cohesive plan, with blocks that help the eye travel over and around the design.

Quilt Finishing

When your blocks are arranged to your satisfaction, it is time to sew them together, add borders as desired, and finish the quilt. For more information on borders, quilting designs, and labels, see "Finishing Up," beginning on page 95.

Isn't it wonderful to own an Around-the-Block quilt? Now you are a Passionate Picture Producer and a Creative Collage Collaborator!

Around the Island by Sara Jane Perino, 1993, Pullman, Washington, 42" x 50". A family vacation inspired this lovely quilt, and Janie's friends dreamed of exotic locations while making their blocks.

Sample Group Guidelines

Stitch 'n Study Quilt Group
Pullman, Washington

Patchin' People Quilt Guild has several small groups, one of which is the Stitch 'n' Study group. The members of this group are often guinea pigs for Pat and Donna's ideas for new projects and classes! Eleven quilters signed up to be the first people to try their most recent brainstorm—the Around-the-Block Round Robin quilt project.

We drew names out of a hat for the rotation order. The first exchange was on April 9, 1993. We exchanged projects every two weeks and returned them to their owners four months later in August. Participants really liked the two-week time schedule. Projects were part of show-and-tell at every meeting. Owners could comment and give guidelines for future additions and other participants also offered suggestions. The makers could listen to all the free advice and then do their own thing if they wanted.

The group felt that being able to see the projects ahead of time and hear each other's comments helped the creative process, particularly since the time schedule was short. A reunion party was held with spouses and guests. After a potluck meal, the completed quilts were unveiled during show-and-tell.

Quiltmakers who participated in this project are: Kathleen H. Butts, "Passion for Paisley" (page 69); Eleanor Kiser Cole, "Orient on My Mind" (page 64) ; Rose Marie Shields Ferner, "Living or Survival" (page 73); Judy Hopkins, "Starry Starry Night" (page 70) ; Pat Maixner Magaret, "Go Tell It on the Mountain" (page 73); Sara Jane Perino, "Around the Island" (page 75); Shirley Perryman, "All Aboard" (page 69); Lee Ellen Philpott, "Dutch Winds Stir My Soul" (page 71); Jeanie Ware Renfro, "Polar Bear Alert" (page 72); Donna Ingram Slusser, "McSlusser's Garden" (page 74); Sharon Heslop Wiser, "Games People Play" (page 72)

Around-the-Block Rules

1. Mark a grid of 4" squares on a large piece of Pellon® fleece with a permanent marker. Make the total grid size 8 squares x 10 squares.
2. Make a theme block, 16" x 16" or 12" x 20" (finished size). Pin or baste this block anywhere on the gridded fleece. This is where it will remain during the entire progressive design process. If your design is a rectangle, decide whether it will be placed on the horizontal or vertical. Then label the top edge of the fleece by writing "top" with a pen.
3. Prepare a traveling box. Include up to 2 yards of assorted fabrics and ½ yard of the background fabric, which can be one or several fabrics. Also send along a journal and a label if you wish. Include resource materials and information explaining your theme and suggestions about related motifs.
4. Always pass your project box to the next person on your list.
5. When you receive a quilt top, make enough blocks to cover six squares on the grid. Make one to two special accent blocks that carry out the theme. Then make four to five simple spacer blocks.
6. You may combine squares to make a larger block, for example, 4" x 8" or even 8" x 8", but don't make too many of these for a quilt. Ask the owner if you have questions.
7. Use only block designs that are four-patch units. Pin your blocks anywhere on the grid.
8. Participants can use up to three of their own fabrics. (We threw out this rule after the first rotation!)
9. It is OK to duplicate other participants' blocks if they will enhance the design.
10. Hide your initials on the front of each block you make. Use a Pigma pen.
11. After your project is returned, you have the option of rearranging existing blocks and adding more. Additional borders and methods of finishing the quilt are also at your discretion.
12. *Accuracy* is extremely important. All blocks must measure 4½" x 4½", unfinished. The owner may decide not to include inaccurate or distorted blocks.

Around-the-Block Formats

> ## ↩ Note
>
> All grids shown require 4" x 4" blocks (finished). The total number of blocks to be made does not always divide evenly among the participants. The owner makes the extra blocks after the final rotation.
>
> The shaded area in each format represents the theme block.

5 blocks x 7 blocks

Number of participants: 5
Theme block size:
  12" x 12" (finished)
Finished size of top:
  20" x 28"
Size of designing wall:
  24" x 32"
Each participant makes:
  6 supporting blocks
Owner makes:
  theme block and 2 supporting blocks

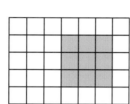

5 block x 7 block format

6 blocks x 7 blocks

Number of participants: 6
Theme block size:
  12" x 12" (finished)
Finished size of top:
  24" x 28"
Size of designing wall:
  28" x 32"
Each participant makes:
  6 supporting blocks
Owner makes:
  theme block and 3 supporting blocks

6 block x 7 block format

6 blocks x 8 blocks

Number of participants: 7
Theme block size:
  12" x 12" finished
Finished size of top:
  24" x 32"
Size of designing wall:
  28" x 36"
Each participant makes:
  6 supporting blocks
Owner makes:
  theme block and 3 supporting blocks

6 block x 8 block format

7 blocks x 9 blocks

Number of participants: 8
Theme block size:
  16" x 16" (finished)
Finished size of top:
  28" x 36"
Size of designing wall:
  32" x 40"
Each participant makes:
  6 supporting blocks
Owner makes:
  theme block and 5 supporting blocks

7 block x 9 block format

7 blocks x 10 blocks

Number of participants: 9
Theme block size:
  16" x 16" (finished)
Finished size of top:
  28" x 40"
Size of designing wall:
  32" x 44"
Each participant makes:
  6 supporting blocks
Owner makes:
  theme block and 6 supporting blocks

7 block x 10 block format

8 blocks x 9 blocks

Number of participants: 10
Theme block size:
  16" x 16" (finished)
Finished size of top:
  32" x 36"
Size of designing wall:
  36" x 40"
Each participant makes:
  6 supporting blocks
Owner makes:
  theme block and 2 supporting blocks

8 block x 9 block format

8 blocks x 10 blocks

8 block x 10 block format

Number of participants: 11
Theme block size:
  16" x 16" (finished)
Finished size of top:
  32" x 40"
Size of design wall:
  36" x 44"
Each participant makes:
  6 supporting blocks
Owner makes:
  theme block and 4
  supporting blocks

8 blocks x 11 blocks

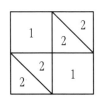

8 block x 11 block format

Number of participants: 12
Theme block size:
  16" x 16" (finished)
Finished size of top:
  32" x 44"
Size of design wall:
  36" x 48"
Each participant makes:
  6 supporting blocks
Owner makes:
  theme block and 6
  supporting blocks

Spacer Blocks

Full-size templates for these blocks appear on pages 124–127. *An R following the template number indicates that you must turn the template over and cut a reverse (mirror image) of the original shape.*

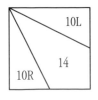

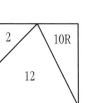

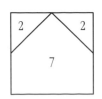

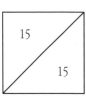

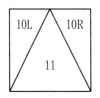

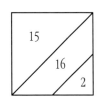

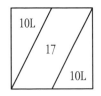

Round Robin Variations

The Round Robin method can be adapted to other quilting projects. Quilters have utilized fun and inventive ways for working on friends' projects. What other Round Robin quilt ideas are waiting out there to be developed? We love to hear about your adaptations and the resulting projects. Here are two that involve wearable art instead of quilts.

The Quilt Guild
of Greater Victoria, Texas

Round Robin Friendship Jackets

Judy Murrah, author of *Jacket Jazz*, inspired eighteen members who had previously made wearable art jackets in her classes to participate in this Round Robin project. Wonderful Friendship jackets, kept secret from their owners until a special unveiling, resulted from this six-month labor of love. Using what they had learned in Judy's classes and from her book, each participant made the patchwork back for her own jacket and placed

Six Friends by Judy Murrah and friends, 1993, Victoria, Texas. A symphony of colors splash across this classic jacket shape. It's a show stopper in any crowd!

"The Friendship Jacket Round Robin was great fun for nineteen willing quilters. Some participants agonized the whole month over each jacket part, asking for advice and approval from other stitchers. Other participants welcomed each challenge, moved quickly, and completed their jacket parts in a matter of hours. Exchanging jacket boxes each month was charged with lots of excitement and apprehension. After six months passed and the completed jackets were revealed, everyone praised the results but breathed a sigh of relief that it was over. Each one liked what had been done to the jacket they started and so faithfully passed on to other friends."

Judy Murrah

"You couldn't help but think about the person on whose jacket you were working during the whole month. I treasure the jacket, but the friendships are the real treasure of this project. (The first friend who worked on my jacket has asked that it be left to her in my will!)"

Michelle Goodson

it in a box along with fabrics. "Bribes," such as little gifts, tea bags, and fun books, were included for encouragement and inspiration. Judy designed a lovely Jacket Jazz Journal to include in each box.

Judy's letter with pertinent project information and group guidelines appears on page 81. It is a good model to follow when giving out necessary information at the beginning of a project. Judy also wrote letters during the duration of the project. These included words of encouragement, an inspirational poem on friendship, a clever listing of participants with their projects and bribes, as well as reminders of important dates.

The last person to receive the jacket in the final rotation was responsible for finishing the jacket, rather than adding to it. It was unveiled to the owner just before she modeled it as part of a style show at a guild meeting.

Quilters who worked on both these projects are: Liz Coles, Michelle Goodson, Lucy Koonce, Edna LaFour, Judy Murrah, Mary Ann Sebolt, and Frances Strauss.

A Celebration by Michelle Goodson and friends, 1993, Victoria, Texas. Butterflies, textures, and party colors accent this festive jacket.

March 8, 1993

Dear Friend,

So glad you are one of the 18 people who has decided to participate with me in the Friendship Jacket Exchange. If you haven't already done so, it's time to get your Friendship Jacket materials together. I've had a lot of fun playing with choosing my fabrics, embellishments, and the design for the back, which will ultimately be the design for Jacket Seven in the new book, *Jacket Jazz Encore*. I can't wait to see all of yours.

These are the dates to keep posted through the end of August:

March 18: Bring your jacket box to my house. Your box should contain:

1. A jacket foundation with the fronts sewed to the jacket back at the shoulder seams only. Sleeves should be separate. The major part of the jacket back should be covered with your patchwork or fabric manipulation. For ideas, see your jacket class notes and *Jacket Jazz*, or create one of your own.

2. An assortment of 8–10 fabrics for other patchwork and fabric manipulations for your jacket. These should be in $1/4$ yd.- to $1/2$ yd.-pieces.

3. The lining cut out with fronts sewn to the back at the shoulders and sleeves separate.

4. Trim for finishing the seams: 6–10 yards of gimp, braid, or piping or an assortment of several different types.

5. Thread to match the main fabric color(s).

6. Any decorative threads, buttons, trinkets, beads, etc., you would like used on your jacket.

7. Any bribes to entice your friends to do a spectacular and creative job on your jacket.

8. Your journal. On the introduction page, feel free to make specific requests for your jacket. However, there are no rules that say your requests must be honored. Write whatever you want on this first page. The journal will be passed on with your jacket to each person listed on your box top. Each month you will receive another journal belonging to the friend whose jacket you receive for that month. Please enter your thoughts, drawings, photos, snippets, or whatever you feel is appropriate. Make these journals fun and interesting as we'll display them at the August meeting for the guild members.

March 25: Jacket boxes will be passed out to each of the participants. A list of who gets each box and in what order will be taped to the top of the box. This will be the only meeting during which each of the jackets will be revealed to the membership until the finale meeting in August. It's OK to give members a peek into the box you have at meetings after this, but don't let the original owner see hers. It's a secret.

April 22: Return box with right jacket front completed. Take home a third box.

May 27: Return box with left jacket front completed. Take home a fourth box.

June 24: Return box with right jacket sleeve completed. Take home a fifth box.

July 22: Return box with left jacket sleeve completed. Take home a sixth box.

August 26: Return box with jacket constructed, lined, and ready to wear. Present jacket to its original owner. Be prepared to receive *your* jacket and model it in the finale of the style show.

August 30: Attend Friendship Jacket Alum luncheon at my house to swap stories about the fun you had with each jacket.

I am so excited to get started. See you on the 18th.

Your friend,
Judy Murrah

The Garment Groupies
Fairbanks, Alaska

"It was interesting, exciting, and scary to watch your project fabric piece change each month. I didn't always like what I saw. You have no control over what other people do to your initial work. But, I love the finished product!"

Corlis Taylor

"I really enjoyed being surprised each month by what had been done to our quilt tops. It was truly a lesson in trust!"

Gayle Murray Hazen

Round Robin Project Rules

1. Place a quilt block or fat quarter of fabric in a paper bag.
2. Take someone else's bag home and work on that project for a month. Add at least 2" to the block. You can slash and insert fabric to your heart's content. Bring the changed project in an anonymous paper bag to the next meeting.
3. Projects will be photographed at the meeting. They will then be returned to the bags and exchanged again.
4. When your quilt top is returned to you after the last exchange, take it home and make a vest.

This group of friends used the anonymous Brown Bag or Paper Bag format. They enjoyed the opportunity to work with colors they might not have chosen for their own garments. Their "slash and sew" rule gave them the freedom to do wild and crazy things to each other's projects. They became very adventurous, slashing blocks in pieces and sewing them back together again with other fabrics to create a new look.

Monthly meetings included demonstrations of techniques, plus critiques and discussions of the evolving projects. They enjoyed this exchange so much that they have completed a second Round Robin project that resulted in various quilted clothing items. They have also completed a third project, which could be made into anything the owner wanted to make.

After the first exchange, they felt rules should be set prior to the beginning of the project, such as how much larger the block should be made during each rotation. Another suggestion was to have a set rotation order so you don't get the same bag twice.

While Gayle Hazen was working on these projects, her daughter, Meredith, became intrigued with wearable art and wanted a vest of her own. Gayle used the leftover scraps from her finished project to make a vest for Meredith. The result shows how one quilter used her creativity to make a family member feel a part of Mom's quilting world.

The finished vests have been exhibited as a group at Patchwork and Pinafores in Rochester, Minnesota. They were also selected through a portfolio review to be part of the exhibit "Beyond the Fig Leaf, An Exhibition of Contemporary Clothing and Accessories" at the Fairbanks Civic Center Gallery in May 1994.

The vest owned by Corlis Taylor is shown on page 83. Persons who also worked on this vest were: Elizabeth Shapland, Susan Dillinger, MaryBeth Smetzer, Gayle Hazen, and Jamie DeVries.

"I Want One Like Mom's," made by Gayle Murray Hazen and owned by Meredith Claire Hazen, is shown on page 83. Persons who also worked on this project were Suzanne Carroll, Isa Smith, Corlis Taylor, and Jamie DeVries.

Vest by Corlis Taylor, 1993, Fairbanks, Alaska. This fun vest has a Crazy-quilt look made elegant with the use of lamé and special fabrics.

I Want One Like Mom's by Gayle Murray Hazen, 1993, Fairbanks, Alaska. Using scraps left over from her own Round Robin vest project, Gayle made a child's version for her daughter. She added sewing motifs as embellishments. (Owned by Meredith Hazen.)

Stitch 'n Study

Pullman, Washington

Sometimes a quilt combines the best features of the traditional Friendship quilts and the Round Robin format. This group made an Opportunity quilt for their city as a fund-raising project to host the Washington State Games during the summer of 1993. They made a basic sketch of the state of Washington and divided it into sections. Color and the basics of good design, such as scale, unity, and balance, were considered. Participants each worked on their individual sections in the manner of making traditional Friendship quilts. They passed the quilt around the group Round-Robin style as members sewed the project together, added mountain ranges and other geographical features, sewed on the borders, and then quilted the project. The original idea to use this wall hanging as an Opportunity quilt was changed. Instead, posters were made of this quilt, and the revenue from their sales helped sponsor the games.

"The Wonders of Washington" is the result of this project, and it is owned by the Department of Parks and Recreation, City of Pullman, Washington.

Those who worked on this project are: Eleanor Kiser Cole, Rose Marie Shields Ferner, Pat Maixner Magaret, Sara Jane Perino, Shirley Perryman, Lee Ellen Philpott, Jeanie Ware Renfro, Donna Ingram Slusser, Daleah Thiessen, and Sharon Heslop Wiser.

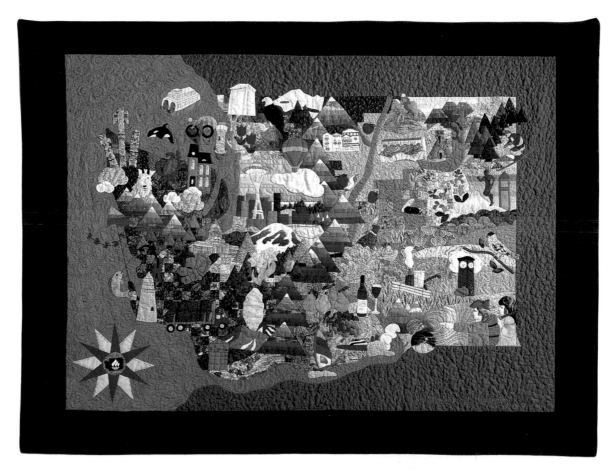

Wonders of Washington by Stitch 'n Study, 1993, Pullman, Washington, 62" x 47". This quilt shows the many attractions found in the state of Washington. (Owned by the City of Pullman, Department of Parks and Recreation. Photo by Marc LaMareaux.)

Design Basics

Quilts have become an art form. Therefore, good quilt design depends on the same criteria that apply to any unified design. Don't let yourself be intimidated or overwhelmed by phrases like "basic principles of art" or "basic elements of design," even if you don't have any formal art training. You have used some of these principles and ideas before.

Webster defines design as a "plan or sketch" or "to prepare the preliminary sketch or the plans for (a work to be executed)." Another word for design is composition, which Webster defines as "the organization or grouping of different parts of a work of art so as to achieve a unified whole." These definitions both imply careful selection and arrangement rather than a random, haphazard placement of items.

Information about the basic elements of design and the principles of art appears in this chapter to help you plan or add to various quiltmaking projects, particularly the Add-On Appliqué and Around-the-Block projects. Consider this a basic summary; for additional information on design, check your local library for comprehensive books on the design process.

Designing is solving a visual problem. You start with a blank space. How do you want to fill that space? What do you want to communicate? How will you arrange or organize the various objects and shapes within the space to express your thoughts and ideas? As you ponder these questions, remember that there are usually several solutions, not just one. However, there are general rules and guidelines to help make the final decisions.

As you review the design guidelines, remember that you can push the rules. "Rules are made to be broken," is a phrase commonly heard in art circles. This does not mean that anything goes or that every design is a good design. It's important to understand the basic concepts and, at the same time, be willing to experiment and try new ideas. Most important, trust your own common sense and good judgment.

Using the basic elements and principles of design is similar to preparing food. To make a successful dish, you prepare specific amounts of required ingredients in the manner given in the recipe. Hopefully, the finished item closely resembles the desired product! For example, Pat combines chocolate, milk, and frozen yogurt to create a delicious chocolate milkshake. Sometimes she adds new ingredients, such as nuts and candies. Donna changes the ingredients by deleting chocolate and adding fresh fruit, preferably peaches.

Changing the ingredients and their amounts obviously changes the character and flavor of the milkshakes. If we leave the ingredients the same but combine them in a different manner, we have a different food item.

We can refer to the basic elements of design as ingredients—line, shape, color, value, texture, and space. They are essential ingredients to all designs. They can be combined in many different ways to create a good design. The principles of design are unity, emphasis, balance, scale, and rhythm. They refer to how the elements are combined and what proportions are used to create a pleasing design. It is not necessary to use every element (ingredient) or every principle (method of combining) in every design.

The Elements of Design

Line

Line refers to a mark or stroke and has unlimited possibilities for expression. Line brings energy to a design and has movement and direction. Vertical lines give the feeling of strength, elevation, and formality. They lead the eye up or down. Horizontal lines are casual and calm. They move the eye across the design. Diagonal lines are energetic and forceful. They add excitement and tension. Curved lines give the impression of flowing grace. Meandering lines help the eye follow a path. Use lines that emphasize the content and feelings you want to convey.

Shape

When a line moves around and then comes back to meet its starting point, it makes a flat, enclosed form—a shape. All of the images we put in our quilts are shapes or are made up of an arrangement of shapes. When looking at images, see if you can discover a basic shape. Is it circular or elliptical? Rectangular or square?

In quiltmaking, you must consider the shapes within the composition, as well as the overall basic shape, and outer dimensions of the quilt. Choose a shape that best expresses what you want to portray—square, rectangular, circular, oval, or hexagonal, for example. In some Round Robin quilts, the owner of the finished quilt top does not always have total control of the final shape. The Border Beauties and Around-the-Block quilts may start their journeys as one shape and end up as another. In the Add-On Appliqué projects, the owner has control of the shape.

The square and the rectangle are the most common formats in quiltmaking. The rectangle can be placed so it is either vertical or horizontal. If the design is a vertical rectangle, the eye naturally moves up and down. To enhance this shape and the natural eye movement it creates, choose design elements with the same tall look, such as tall trees or a vase of flowers.

The horizontal rectangle encourages the eye to move across the design. This shape is conducive to spreading designs, such as landscapes. The square format does not move the eye and is restful or static. It is a little more difficult to make an exciting, yet unified, square design.

Color

Color is the single most important element in determining the overall effect of a design. It is probably the first thing noticed by the viewer. There are many ways to describe the properties of color and their effects in a composition.

✍ A Note about the Creative Process

When planning a design for an entire project or adding borders or motifs to a project, there is a creative process involved that can't be rushed. Allow time for thinking, visualizing, drawing, sketching, and planning. Experiment with the elements of design, such as different lines and shapes. Vary the placement of the focal point.

As you sketch, remember to use both ends of your pencil. Use the lead at one end to add lines and the eraser at the other end to create wonderful spaces. Try a variety of possibilities. Explore and let ideas develop; don't stop with the first idea that comes to mind. It is easier to work with many designs during the selection process.

1. Create as many designs as you can.
2. Eliminate the designs that are definitely not right for this project.
3. Separate the designs that might work from the ones that you like best.
4. Make the final selection.
5. Save all other designs in a notebook for future projects.

- *Hue* is the name given to a color, such as red, blue, yellow.
- *Value* refers to the lightness or darkness of a color.
- *Intensity* indicates brightness or dullness of a color.
- *Temperature* pertains to the warmth or coolness of a color. If a color wheel is positioned so that yellow is at the top, all the colors on one side of it contain red and are warm. The colors on the other side of the color wheel contain blue and are cool.

Colors give a mood or feeling to a design. Warm colors are lively while cool colors are calming. Intense colors are healing while dull colors are conservative, stable, and dreamlike. Certain colors dominate and it is best to use less of these. For example, use less of bright and warm colors unless creating a special effect. A little goes a long way.

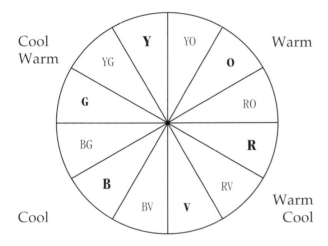

Generally, it is best if one color family dominates a design. If two strong colors are used in equal amounts, a strong negative tension is created. Learn to use color contrasts to your advantage. A bright spot might jazz up an otherwise dull design. Use it as an accent.

Value

Value is one of the properties of color mentioned above. However, it is important enough to include more information about it here.

Value is used by artists to describe the comparative lightness or darkness of a color. There is an infinite number of value degrees between very, very light and very, very dark within each color family.

Value is relative. The value of an area (or a piece of fabric) depends upon the value of the colors that surround it. Value is used to create moods and feelings, space and depth, volume and roundness, illusions and special effects. It is used in a variety of ways that depend upon *contrast*.

Contrast in value refers to the interaction or relationship between areas of light and dark. Low-value contrast refers to similar values used together in a composition. When the values are mostly light, you create an uplifting, ethereal feeling. Using mostly dark values creates a somber, heavy, even mysterious mood. When similar values are used together, the edges of objects are blurred, and a subdued, calm, muted feeling is created.

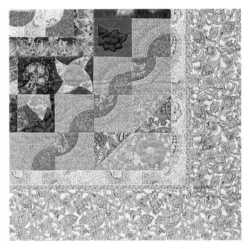

Passion for Paisley, page 69

When you combine extreme lights and darks together in a composition, the result is high contrast. High contrast makes a dramatic and forceful statement, creating tension and excitement in a design. Areas of sunlight and shadow found in nature are examples of high contrast.

Courtyard of Roses, page 54

All My Quilting Friends Are Stars, page 55

Creating a three-dimensional effect from lines and flat planes involves subtle shifts in value. This gives dimension to objects and shapes.

Texture

Texture is the visual design element that indicates surface structure. Texture provides interest and gives life to quilts. Fabric gives the quiltmaker instant texture. Some fabrics actually have a tactile and visual texture, such as smooth, rough, or soft. Satin is smooth and shiny; wool can be smooth or fuzzy; corduroy is soft; organdy is crisp and sheer.

More commonly in quiltmaking, the surface design printed on the fabrics provides visual texture. We are alerted to certain sensations, even though we may not actually touch the fabric surface. Memory provides the clues that allow us to visually enjoy the texture presented on the surface. For example, some prints look like wood grain, real flowers, rocks, or ocean waves.

Surface embellishments and quilting add to this quality. When using texture, it is best to vary patterned and quiet areas in order to provide a resting place for the viewer's eye.

Use value contrast to emphasize the center of interest or focal point of the design. For example, you immediately notice an object that is light in value when it is placed on a relatively dark background.

Value contrast is also used to suggest space and depth. Your eyes naturally view images as becoming grayer and less distinct the farther they recede into the distance. This effect of depth can be duplicated by manipulating the values in designs. See Aerial Perspective on page 89.

Selecting prints that resemble the texture of stones gives a realistic appearance to the garden pathway. From *Secret Garden*, page 50.

Space

Space is the total area of a design (length x width). Objects and images in the design take up space. They are considered positive. The empty spaces between and around these images are called negative spaces. Positive and negative spaces should relate to one another.

Do not think of negative space as wasted space. It is just as important as the positive space. For example, a poorly designed and executed background contributes nothing to the subject or point of interest. Sometimes, the relationship between the positive and negative spaces is not clear, and the eye must work hard to find the relationship between the two. In such a situation, there is constant movement and change without the unity necessary to hold the viewer's attention.

The illusion of depth or distance in our designs depends upon creating a working relationship between the positive and negative spaces. The following factors can be used to achieve this effect. Refer to the illustration.

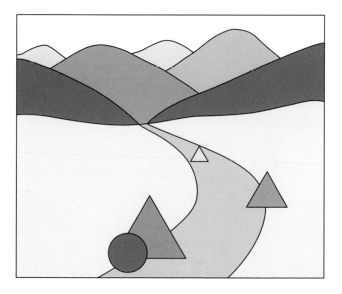

Size. When we look into the distance, images appear to look smaller the farther away they are. We know that the trees in the distance are similar in size to those that are close, even though they appear smaller. Achieve depth by making faraway objects smaller.

Overlapping. When a shape covers or hides part of another object, it creates an illusion of depth. The images that are partially covered appear to be farther away.

Linear Perspective. This describes what happens when parallel lines seem to converge as they approach the horizon. This effect is commonly seen when railroad tracks, a meandering stream, or a road moves from the foreground to the background, getting narrower and narrower as it seemingly disappears into the distance. Size helps create this effect.

Aerial Perspective. Color, value, and intensity can all combine to indicate depth. Colors seem to change as you look into the distance. The farther the objects recede, the less distinct and bright the images appear. Up close, shapes are brighter, and detail, dimension, contour, and texture are more obvious. Distant images have more muted colors that often take on a bluish tinge. Details are blurred and objects look flat and smooth. Objects that are closer seem to have high-value contrast between lights and darks, highlights and shadows. Distant shapes appear to have similar values. Achieve this effect in designs by using a variety of value changes and contrasts.

Vertical Location. Depth can also be achieved by placing images another way. Closer objects are set lower, closer to the bottom of the design. Far objects are set higher up, closer to the horizon line.

The Principles of Design

The elements of design are the individual ingredients used in the recipe for a design. Next, you need the principles of design—guidelines for combining them to create a pleasing composition.

Unity (Harmony)

Unity refers to the planned arrangement of the various elements in a visually pleasing manner. This means that the different parts of the design appear to belong to each other in some manner and tie together visually. Harmony results when the total visual effect is greater than the parts. A design has unity when the viewer notices the overall effect, a thread that binds everything together, rather than individual pieces with no relationship.

When harmony is achieved, movement develops. The eye moves around the design as the relationship between the elements becomes obvious. When elements are not unified or harmonious, trouble spots stop the eye and prevent it from following the design in a rhythmic pattern. The various forms and elements of the design appear separate and unrelated if there is no unity.

There is a variety of ways to create unity, and you may find that certain ones are more natural to your personal style than others.

Proximity. This is the easiest way to achieve unity. Move individual elements close together to make them look as if they belong to one another. The eye moves smoothly from one element, then on to the next, without jumping around and losing interest.

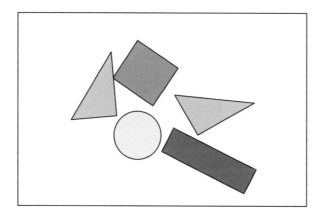

Unity achieved by proximity

Repetition. Repeat elements or objects in the design so the eye moves across the design, creating unity. Rhythm (page 94) is related to repetition.

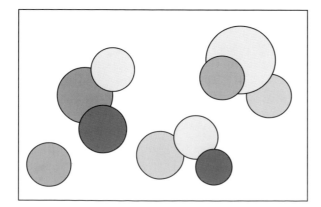

Unity achieved by repetition

Variety. When elements are repeated, they must be varied, or the design becomes static and boring.

Unity achieved by repetition and variety

Too much variety creates an unplanned and uncontrolled feeling. Strive for repetition with a balance of variety to make the design pleasing to the eye.

Continuation. Place the various shapes so that the edge of one naturally leads into another. The eye then flows easily from one to the next.

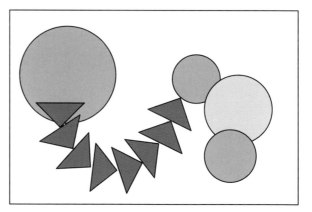

Unity achieved by continuation

Contrast. Create interest by using contrast. (Refer to more information about contrast on page 93). It is usually necessary for shapes to show up against the background or against other shapes. When contrast is high, it shows strength and attracts the attention of the viewer. Tension develops between opposing elements. Each "push-and-pull" gives energy to the design.

Contrast does not always need to be high, however. Subtlety can speak just as loudly. If contrast is low, the shape's lines and edges are muted and might even melt into the background or other shapes. Sometimes you might want this effect.

Learn to control contrasts to make them work for you. Some examples of contrast to consider as you plan a design include:

- curved lines and shapes against straight ones (See "Secret Garden" on page 50.)
- light and dark values next to each other (See "To Market to Market" on page 53.)
- a small shape against or in front of a large shape (See "The Nutcracker" on page 57.)
- contrasting shapes next to each other (See "I Can't Believe It's Mine" on page 52.)
- vertical lines crossing horizontal lines (See "Flora, Fauna, and Friends" on page 60.)
- simple versus decorative (See "Gracious Generosity" on page 21.)
- complementary colors near each other (See "Around the Island" on page 75.)
- warm and cool colors next to each other (See "Midnight Sunflower" on page 53.)
- dull and bright colors near each other (See "Full Circle" on page 51.)

Emphasis

This is the center of interest or focal point. It tells the story and sets the theme. We all want people to take time to look at our quilts a first time and we want them to be worthy of a second look, and another and another. The focal point attracts the viewer's eye and invites further attention.

Sometimes you'll find more than one area of emphasis. Generally, these are supporting images that carry out the central theme or idea. They are accents or secondary focal points. One focal point with several secondary images makes an interesting design. However, be careful not to create a cluttered design with too many areas of interest.

A good rule to follow is: Don't tell too many stories in one design. One object or shape should dominate with the rest being subordinate. The eye is naturally selective and cannot focus on too many things at once. Use moderation in the design's interest area. Don't make it too strong or it will seem unnatural. Remember, when everything is emphasized, nothing is emphasized.

Sometimes, the artist creates no focal point in the design. The viewer is invited to look at the assorted images and objects and discover their intriguing importance and how they are connected to each other. For example, "Starry Starry Night" on page 70 has many attractive elements that challenge us to discover their relationship.

Guidelines for Creating Design Emphasis

If there are several focal points to position, try following several of the options discussed below. When using any of these methods, don't try to be too exact. Eyeball the design, apply the different options, and make a decision based on your own good design sense.

> ### ✎ Tip
>
> When you are placing shapes in the design, odd numbers of objects are visually more pleasing or interesting than even numbers.

Subject Matter. The choice of subject matter itself may create emphasis. For example, people or faces in a design invite the viewers to relate to the subject matter since they are also members of the human race.

Placement of Subject Matter. Shapes and objects can be arranged in a variety of ways to create emphasis. Don't be tempted to place the focal point in the exact center of the design. It will definitely be noticed there, but it may have more interest if placed elsewhere. Several options are discussed and illustrated below. Shapes in the following illustrations represent either single objects or grouped objects.

Offset. If the design is divided in half both vertically and horizontally, try creating the focal point in one of the quadrants about halfway between the center and one of the corners. There are four choices.

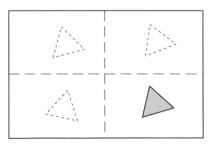

Quarters. Divide the longer direction of the design into four equal imaginary sections. Place the center of interest on one of the outer quarter lines. There are two options.

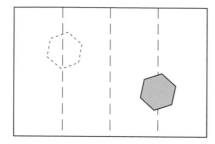

Ninepatch. Using the same technique as above, divide the design into thirds, both vertically and horizontally. Place the area of emphasis near one of the intersections. There are four options available.

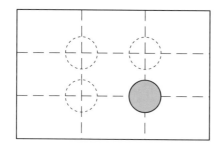

Triangle. Use this method when there are three objects to position. Draw an imaginary triangle within the design and place the centers of interest near the triangle points. Orient the triangle any way you wish within the outer boundaries of the composition.

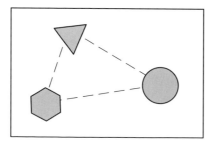

Diagonal Line. A diagonal line in a design can emphasize it. However, if there is no subtle effect or shape to counterbalance the strength of the diagonal line, the viewers eye goes beyond the outer edges of the design. "Escape to Amorgas" on page 63 originally had a diagonal

road that was very strong until other objects were placed on the quilt top.

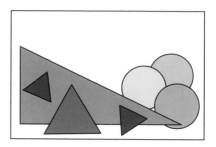

Letters. Objects and shapes can be arranged to form a letter, such as an "O," "U," "L," or "S"(below). These interest areas create movement and lead the eye across and around the design.

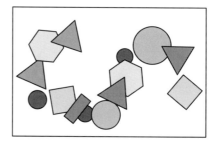

The Cross. A strong vertical line crossing a horizontal area creates a focal point.

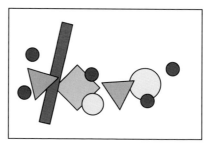

Isolation. If most of the shapes and images in the design are together in one area, but one image is alone or isolated, the eye is attracted to this single image as a point of interest.

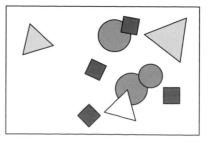

Grouped Objects. Clustering objects in a group can create the main point of interest. They are often placed on a relatively simple background. Many still-life and floral paintings exhibit this type of emphasis.

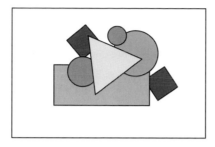

Pointers. Arrange some of the elements so they point to other elements. Lines that radiate from a central shape lead the eye back to the center of interest. If you are walking down the street and notice that someone is looking up at the sky, chances are, you will look up, too. You can create pointers in your quilt designs, too, by adding objects or lines that look at, face, or point to the object you want to emphasize in your design.

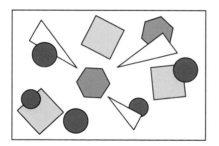

Lighting. You can emphasize the focal point in a design by positioning it in a lighter area of the design. This is like using a spotlight for stage lighting.

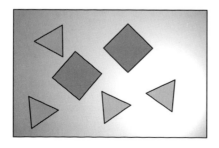

Contrast. If the elements in the focal point differ from the other elements in the design, the eye is drawn to it. Perhaps the color of the focal point is different from colors elsewhere. Maybe all the images in the design are larger than the subject. Contrasts make the viewer take notice.

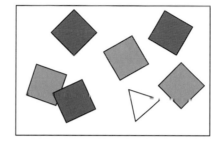

Balance

Balance is the distribution of elements throughout the design in such a way that equilibrium is achieved. Balance is not necessarily determined by the size of the images and elements, but by their visual weight. Symmetry is part of the concept of balance. To understand this concept, visualize an imaginary line placed on the vertical through the center of the design.

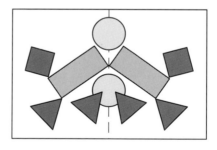

When you compare both sides of the line or axis and find that they are mirror images of each other, the design has bilateral symmetry. If the top and bottom of the design are not also identical, keep more weight toward the bottom of the design rather than at the top. "Secret Garden" on page 50 is a good example of bilateral symmetry.

Now imagine two dividing lines, one vertical and one horizontal, through the center of the design. If the elements in all four quadrants are identical, the design has radial symmetry.

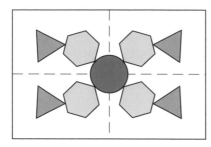

With all symmetrically balanced designs, the mood is relaxed and solid. The eye travels across the design and always comes back to the center. Many quilt designs are symmetrical in nature. "Gee, What a Great Group" on page 54 is a good example of a symmetrical design.

Designs can also be asymmetrical. These are usually more exciting and less predictable. In an asymmetrical design, the elements and images are not the same on both sides of the axis. Remember, the size of the elements is not necessarily the factor to consider when establishing balance. Visual weight or impact is what needs to be balanced. A small shape of an eye-catching color may balance a larger shape of a dull or neutral color. A small, irregular-shaped image may balance a large, regular-shaped image. A small amount of texture might balance a larger shape with no texture.

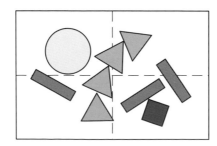

Think of the old-fashioned teeter-totter. It works great if the children at each end are about the same size and weight. What happens if one of the children is larger? What has to happen before they can make the teeter-totter work again? Design balance works in the same manner. Move the elements and images around until everything feels right. Asymmetrical balance is a little more difficult to achieve, but the results can be worth it. "Living in a Material World" on page 22 is a good example of an asymmetrical design.

Scale

Shapes have size and their relationship to each other is called scale. Scale indicates how large or small a shape should be. Since big and small are relative terms, proportion is used to indicate how the images relate to each other and to the whole. Try to keep images in proportion to each other. Are the horse's legs too long for its body? Is the person's head too small? Don't forget, however, that you can create a special effect with unnatural exaggeration. For example, in folk art, a bird and a house might be the same size.

Rhythm

Rhythm is related to repetition. In design, rhythm mainly refers to shapes or lines and the arrangement of repeated motifs throughout the composition in a pattern. Repetition of the same (or very similar) elements provides a feeling of relationship and creative movement. Rhythm can be either regular and systematic or uneven and free-flowing. Refer to "Repetition" on page 90.

Finishing Up

Anonymous

She put so much of herself in this quilt.
Did she laugh with her family,
Have good times with a friend?
Are there smiles stitched in the binding?
Do tears and colors blend?
Was this made for a grandchild,
With patches and scraps of blue?
What is her name, I wonder.
Wistfully, I wish I knew.

Roseanne Lloyd

After the final rotation, each Round Robin project is returned to its owner. It is always a wonderful surprise to see how each beginning block has changed, whether it is a quilt or another type of project. This is the time for another photo session since most of the projects will change again as borders are added and then again when the quilting is completed. Be sure to take photos of individuals and their projects as well as a group shot. If the projects have been kept secret, take photos of each owner as her project is revealed. Videotaping is also a wonderful way to capture excited reactions. Play the tape back at a future get-together for a trip down memory lane.

There is so much excitement after the last rotation that the owners usually can't wait to finish their quilts. With all Round Robin formats, the owner must follow guidelines set for adding, moving, or eliminating motifs, borders, or blocks. Refer to "Design Basics," beginning on page 85, for assistance in making final design decisions that will result in a unified and interesting completed quilt project. (For Round Robin garment projects, use finishing techniques appropriate to the type of clothing.)

Before you finish a quilt top, hang it in a place where you can see it frequently over a period of several days. Observe it in both natural and artificial light. Reflect on ideas for borders, backing fabrics, and quilting lines and make mental or written notes about fabric ideas.

Planning the Borders

Every quilt needs a frame to contain the design elements and to move the eye back into the quilt. If your project doesn't feel finished and begs for a border, examine the quilt photos in this book for ideas and inspiration. They illustrate several different ways to create design interest in the border.

In "McSlusser's Garden" on page 74, the supporting blocks along the edges of the quilt act as a border and make a nice frame for this fun quilt. Another border would be too much.

Sometimes there are leftover blocks that can effectively spill out into the border. This also adds interest to the quilt. In "Polar Bear Alert" on page 72, the squares were rearranged and the large Caution sign and other motifs were moved into the border. The sign suggested the name for this quilt.

Appliquéd elements that spill out into the border also add design interest. In "Flora, Fauna, and Friends" on page 60, an ivy vine meanders into the outer frame.

Use a pieced border that reflects the quilt theme. For example, in "Escape to Amorgas" on page 63, the outer border is composed of the traditional Greek Cross block, reinforcing the theme of the quilt—a vacation to Greece.

Selecting the Border Fabric

Some quilts may only need a simple border composed of a single fabric to provide a frame around the design.

To select a border fabric, take the completed quilt top to your local fabric store and select several bolts of fabric that you think might make an appropriate border. Unroll about one yard from the first bolt and set the quilt on top of it, exposing the prospective border fabric on at least two sides (around a corner). Analyze the color compatibility and degree of "busyness." Try several border widths. Ask yourself the following questions:

⑤ Does this fabric contain the design well?
⑤ Is it too busy or too boring?
⑤ Is it too dark or too light in value?
⑤ Do the colors of this fabric work nicely with those in the quilt top?
⑤ Does it reflect the mood you want your quilt to convey?
⑤ Does it look better as a narrow or as a wide border?

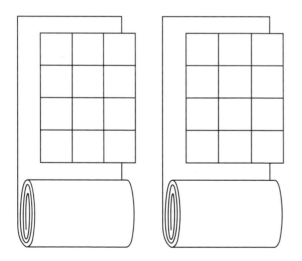

After studying the first prospective border fabric, repeat the process with a second fabric option. Ask yourself the same questions.

Next comes the hard part. Which of the two fabrics looked best with the quilt top? Return the one you like least to the shelf and then choose one or two other fabrics to repeat the test. After each comparison, there will be a winner and a loser. The winner goes on to the next round of competition and the loser goes back to the shelf. After several rounds of the border auditioning process, a "champion" will emerge. Be sure to buy enough fabric for the borders and the method you will use to apply them. We prefer to use the lengthwise grain for borders because of its stability. For additional information on applying borders, see pages 105–7.

Choosing the Backing

Today, many quilts are reversible and "back art" is very popular. Traditional quilts usually have a carefully pieced top and a simple backing. A two-sided or reversible quilt actually has two fronts, with each side carefully planned and interesting in its own right!

Quilters are often tempted to pick up the edge of a quilt to look at the back side. Allow the back of your quilt to be a reflection of the front or let it make an additional statement. Enjoy making "two-fronted" quilts!

Select a backing fabric that reflects the theme of the front or relates to the ideas presented. This carries the flow of the theme nicely from front to back. You can also piece a quilt back to create a design. Plan the piecing to stagger the seams on the back with those on the front whenever possible for minimal bulk.

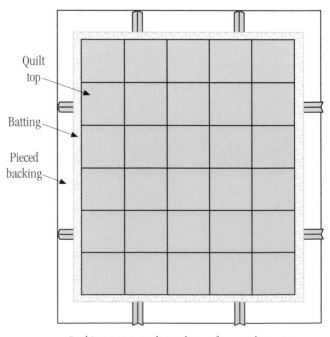

Backing seams are located away from quilt top seams.

If you are a hand quilter, you will probably want to avoid many pieced seams on your backing so needling will be easier. If you are a machine quilter, remember that the electric needle penetrates almost anything, so seams are not a major concern.

In the Around-the-Block Round Robin format, you can use blocks on both sides of the quilt, making the quilt reversible and eliminating hurt feelings.

Two Border Beauties quilts are wonderful examples of how to incorporate the quilt's theme on the back side of the quilt. "All My Quilting Friends Are Stars" has a unique arrangement of blocks by Gayle Noyes that complements the front. Jean VanBockel used fabrics from the front of "Midnight Sunflower" on page 98 to provide a background for the beautiful sunflower on the back. This block was adapted from a Star block on the front of the quilt.

Gayle Noyes effectively arranged extra pieced blocks on the back of her quilt to make it reversible. "All My Quilting Friends Are Stars," page 55.

Planning the Quilting

Select quilting designs that enhance the overall beauty of your quilt. Because of the many seams in these projects, sometimes the best quilting lines are simple ones because they unify the design elements without overpowering them.

In Border Beauties quilts, consider stitching in-the-ditch around some of the pieces or units that should be emphasized, as well as around some of the spacer strips. This makes them pop out and gives them dimension. In some of the open areas, you might choose a fancy quilting pattern that reinforces some area of the center block or medallion. If there is some appliqué in the quilt, echo these lines in another place. In "Gracious Generosity" on page 21, lines from the appliquéd center were repeated as quilting lines in the white outer border.

In Add-On Appliqué and Around-the-Block quilts, you can stitch in-the-ditch around each appliqué motif. Other quilting lines, including straight, curved, flowing, or dramatic, should always emphasize the mood of the quilt.

Do not use a lot of quilting in areas that you want to stand out. Quilt heavily in areas where you want a smoother, flatter effect. Close quilting in the background behind appliquéd motifs helps to make these elements more three-dimensional.

Signing Your Quilt and Adding a Label

Your quilt is an artistic statement and as such, it deserves a name or title and a signature. The quiltmakers who have projects pictured in this book have been clever and sentimental in acknowledging their themes and their friends. Let their titles inspire you!

With Round Robin quilts, it is important to have everyone who participated in making your quilt sign it in some manner. This supports and enhances the notion of a Friendship quilt, and generations from now, your family and quilt historians will thank you.

It is a good idea to ask each participant to initial or sign each border, motif, or block as it is added to a project. This creates a permanent record of who added which border, motif, or block to the quilt. We recommend using a permanent fabric marking tool, such as a Pigma pen.

The owner may also wish to have the people who worked on the project sign the label or the back of the quilt. The Material Girls passed around a piece of muslin for a label with their projects. Each participant signed her name and added a little poetry to each label, creating an autograph album of sorts for the quilts that resulted. The back side of "Living in a Material World" shown below right, is a wonderful example of friendship memories recorded permanently for owner Cynthia Stroo.

There are several options when it comes to labeling your quilt. You may wish to make a label to include in the project box so that each person can sign it as the project is passed around. If the group is large enough, you might want the last participant to make a decorative label rather than adding anything to the quilt top.

The other alternative is for labels to be exchanged Round Robin–style while owners are completing the backing, quilting, and binding.

Whichever method you choose, a label is a way of keeping the history of this quilt with it forever. Your quilt says a lot about you, your friends, and the times in which you live.

Labels can be plain and simple or quite fancy. They provide another opportunity to exercise creativity. The labels described in the following paragraphs depict a variety of styles and methods for including information. Let them be the inspiration for your label on this special Friendship quilt.

In her Add-On Appliqué project, "Amish Summer," shown on page 59, Shirley Perryman designed a small replica of an Amish Bars quilt for the label, shown on page 99. Participants inked their names and listed their additions on the strips. Such a label is a great way to reinforce the theme of the quilt.

Using today's magic machines to design a label is also an option. Lorna Druffel and Chris Schultz asked their brother, Andrew Flack, to design a label on his computer. They took his design to the photocopy shop and had it reduced

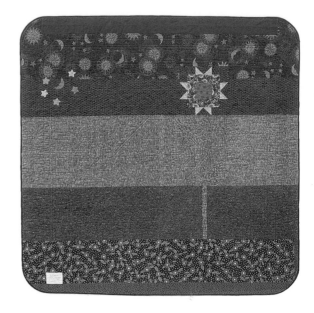

Sunflowers appear on the front and the back of this quilt—and in the garden, too! Back designed and made by Jean Van Bockel. "Midnight Sunflower," page 53.

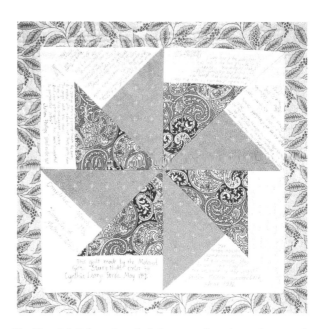

The Material Girls each included a piece of muslin in their traveling boxes for others to document their work on each project. Cynthia incorporated hers into the back of her quilt. "Living in a Material World" by Cynthia Stroo, page 22.

Friends each signed an Amish Bar as the project made its rounds. Shirley made this lovely label to carry out the Amish theme of her quilt. "Amish Summer" by Shirley Perryman, page 59.

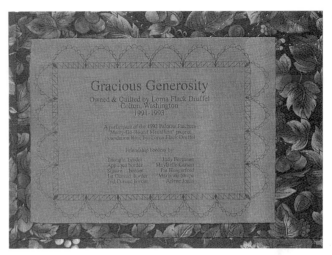

You can use a computer program to design a label and then transfer it to fabric. "Gracious Generosity" by Lorna Flack Druffel, page 21.

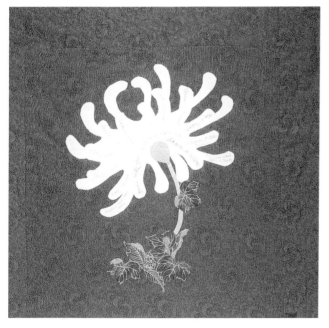

This beautiful label of white chrysanthemum petals effectively carries the theme of the front of the quilt to the back side. "Orient on My Mind" by Eleanor Kiser Cole, page 64.

to the desired size before hand-feeding a stabilized piece of fabric through the copier. Lorna's label is shown above right.

Eleanor Cole had each of her friends sign a different petal on a chrysanthemum blossom. She then incorporated these into a label for the back of "Orient on My Mind," shown at left.

Label Information

In all cases, be sure to include your name as owner and the names of all of the other participants. Include the year the quilt was completed and where the project was made (city and state). If the project traveled from one location to another as it made its rotations, indicate the hometowns of each participant. You might also want to include a note about why the project was made, information about the selected theme, and the project guidelines.

Signing Methods

Choose one of the following methods to record the desired information on the quilt and/or label. First cut the label fabric and stabilize it by ironing the shiny side of a piece of freezer paper to the wrong side. This makes it easier to write, draw, or type on the fabric. After creating the label with any of the methods below, remove the freezer paper, set the ink with a hot iron, and then attach the label to the back of the quilt.

Inking. Use a permanent marking pen, such as a Pigma pen, to write all the pertinent information on the stabilized label fabric. This is a relatively quick and easy way to make a label that records a lot of information in a small space.

Typewriter. Insert the stabilized label fabric into a ribbon-type typewriter. Type all pertinent information onto the fabric.

Computer Printer. Design your label with a computer and a design software program. Stabilize the label fabric, then hand-feed the label through a computer printer that has a ribbon printing system and print your label directly onto the fabric.

Photocopying. Find out if the machines at your local photocopy shop will accept and print on a fabric surface. Ask for their recommendations for preparing your label fabric. Design the label on a computer or by hand (writing and drawing on paper). Take the paper design and stabilized fabric to the photocopy shop and hand-feed the fabric through the machine.

Thermal Image Transfer. You can use this method to transfer not only text but also color drawings and color photos to a fabric surface. It might be fun to take a group photo of your Round Robin participants and include this in the label for your quilt. Contact your local photocopy shop and ask for information about Thermal Image Transfer. In general, this involves making a transparency of your text and/or photo that can be heat transferred to fabric. They can tell you their procedure and make recommendations about preparing the fabric and the label information and/or photo images. Be sure to tell them that you need to have the text reversed so it will not read backwards. This requires an extra step.

"Our project was a wonderful experience for me! It helped me get to know people on a deeper level, something I appreciated since I was somewhat new to the group. I was overwhelmed by the 'Gracious Generosity' poured out to me by the loving handwork people did on my behalf."

Lorna Druffel

"My quilt is named 'To Market to Market,' not only because of the pig in the outer border, but because I did a lot of that! The fabrics I bought did not always work out so I would go back to the shop again!"

Ardell Parkin

Attaching the Label

We think it's a good idea to attach the label to the quilt *before* quilting so the stitches will go through the quilt sandwich and the label, all at the same time. This makes it more difficult to remove and separate the label from the quilt. You can also ink basic information about the quilt directly onto the back of the quilt and then cover it with the label. This is another way of preserving the information and adding a permanent label to the quilt.

Adding a Journal Pocket

If you are afraid your friendship journal that holds the history of your Round Robin quilt will become misplaced, try making a pocket or envelope for it to attach to the back of the quilt. Add a button closure to make sure the journal won't fall out of the pocket.

Quiltmaking Basics

The following pages include basic quiltmaking methods for assembling and finishing your quilt.

Selecting and Preparing Fabric

The best fiber content to use in your projects is 100% cotton. It is durable, handles well, and is easy care. If you use 100% cottons exclusively, all the fabrics in your quilts will age at the same rate. For example, cotton-polyester blends tend to last longer than cotton, and silk disintegrates more quickly.

It is important to prepare and process the fabrics for colorfastness and shrinkage before using them in a project. For colorfastness, test each piece, using our method, or one of your own. To preshrink fabrics, wash and dry them, using the method that works best for you.

How We Prepare Our Fabrics
1. Test for colorfastness by snipping off a small piece of each fabric; wet snippet thoroughly. Do not squeeze out excess water; place on a white paper towel and let dry. Remove from paper towel to see if any dye transferred to the towel.
2. If not colorfast, process fabric with color-setting agents (vinegar or salt) and test again for colorfastness. If the fabric is still not colorfast, do not use it in your quilt.
3. Wash and dry fabric. Iron if necessary.

Fabric Grain Line

Lengthwise grain, crosswise grain, and bias are three terms that describe the direction of the threads in a woven fabric. Lengthwise grain refers to the threads that run parallel to the selvages. If the fabric is pulled on the lengthwise grain, there is almost no "stretch" or "give" to the fabric. This means it is very stable and that is why we prefer to use the lengthwise grain for borders.

Crosswise grain refers to the threads that run across the fabric from selvage to selvage. When the fabric is pulled on the crosswise grain, there is a little "give" to the fabric, more than on the lengthwise grain.

If the fabric is pulled on the diagonal, there is a lot of stretch to it. This diagonal is referred to as the bias, and because fabric cut on the bias can easily stretch out of shape, it is important to be careful when handling bias edges.

You can cut down on stretching problems by placing pattern shapes carefully on the fabric before cutting. It is important that the outside edges of the block are cut on the lengthwise or crosswise grain lines whenever possible so they won't stretch out of shape when you handle them during construction.

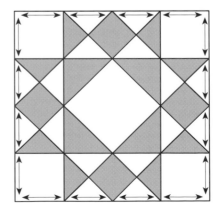

Indicate grain lines on cutting templates by marking arrows on the lengthwise or crosswise grain. When using a rotary cutter, mat, and ruler, be sure the edges of the ruler are parallel to the lengthwise or crosswise grain whenever possible.

Accurate Seaming

Precision piecing is important in creating blocks with accurate measurements. Use a ¼"-wide seam allowance. To ensure that you are sewing ¼"-wide seams, mark an accurate ¼"-wide sewing gauge on your sewing machine.

1. Cut along one of the grid lines on a sheet of accurate graph paper with four squares to the inch.

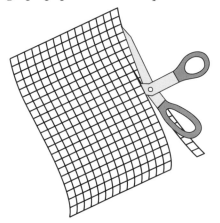

2. Slip the graph paper under the presser foot of your sewing machine, with the cut edge of the paper to the right. Lower the presser foot and needle so that the needle pierces the paper very slightly to the right of the first line on the grid. Place a piece of masking tape right next to the edge of the paper. Remove the paper.

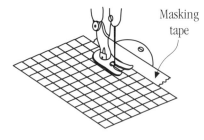

Masking tape

3. Make a ridge to guide the fabric edge by adding several layers of masking tape on top of the first piece, being careful to keep the edges aligned.

4. Set the stitch length on your sewing machine to 12 stitches per inch. Generally, it is not necessary to backstitch at the beginning and end of every seam.

5. When sewing set-in pieces, start and stop the stitching ¼" from the outside edges. Backstitch at both the beginning and end of the seam.

✎ Tip

The distance from the needle to the tape will be a scant ¼" wide because you positioned the needle slightly to the right of the grid line. This is OK, especially when piecing a quilt top with many seams. It makes up for the slight amount of fabric that is lost when you press a seam to one side instead of open as is done in traditional sewing.

Using a Bridge

If you are tired of clipping long threads when sewing projects, try our gizmo, called a *bridge*. To make a bridge, place two rectangles of fabric together (each approximately ¾" x 2"). When it is time to remove the first set of patches from the machine, do not lift the presser foot or clip threads. Instead, run the bridge through the machine; clip the threads at the back of the presser foot, releasing the sewn pieces. When you are ready to begin sewing the next pieces together, ease them under the presser foot without lifting it. Cut the bridge off at the back. This technique saves time and thread.

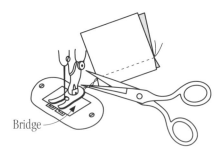

Bridge

Chain Piecing

Chain piecing—sewing pieces together without lifting the presser foot—saves time as well as thread.

1. Sew two pieces together.
2. With the presser foot still down, sew several extra stitches beyond the edge of the fabrics. Do not remove the squares from the machine.
3. Insert another set of pieces under the presser foot and sew them together. Again, sew several stitches beyond the fabric, leaving the presser foot down.
4. Continue inserting new fabrics and "chaining." When you are ready to press the sewn pieces and then join them to the next pieces, clip the threads between pairs to break the chain.

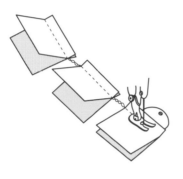

Pressing

Press carefully. We prefer not to use steam until all the pieces have been sewn together to create the quilt top. Set the stitches in each seam after sewing.

1. Place the pieces on the pressing board exactly as they were sewn, right sides together.
2. Press the seam allowances flat, using a lifting, up-and-down motion with the iron. Do not iron the fabrics; it causes stretching and distortion.

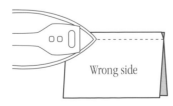

Wrong side

3. After setting the seams, turn the fabrics over to the right side and press the seam allowances to one side.

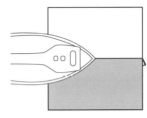

Sewing Units Together

Whenever possible, press the seam allowances so that there will be a seam allowance on each side of the place where seam lines come together. These are "opposing seam allowances" because the seam allowances were pressed in opposite directions; they nestle together easily, and the bulk of the layers is distributed evenly at each seam intersection.

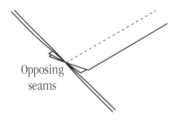

Opposing seams

To ensure precisely matched seams, pin each intersection before sewing. Stitch seams carefully so they are always straight with no gentle curves.

Appliqué

Choose 100% cotton fabric for the appliqués. Cotton is pliable and easy to manipulate. We also prefer to use a two-ply cotton thread for hand sewing the appliqués in place. Match the thread color to the appliqué piece, not to the background.

Use needles called "sharps." They are longer than quilting needles and very slender. Sharps are sized by number: the larger the number, the thinner the needle. Size 12 is the ultimate. The finer the needle, the finer your stitches will be.

Use ½"-long sequin pins to hold the pieces in place on the background. Your sewing thread is less likely to get tangled around these short pins.

Preparing the Appliqués

1. Use a marking tool that leaves marks you can remove easily. Trace the appliqué pattern onto the background fabric to mark the positioning lines for the appliqué pieces.

If the background fabric is light-colored, you can lay it directly over the pattern and see through it well enough to mark the lines. If the background fabric is dark, you may need to use a light box or take the project to a sunny window.

2. Number the pieces in the order they will be appliquéd. Start from the bottom layer, working up. If raw edges can be covered, make sure to appliqué these pieces first.
3. Make templates for each appliqué piece. Trace the shape directly from the pattern sheet or a design you have created yourself. *Do not add seam allowances to the templates.*
4. Place the appliqué templates on the *right side* of the selected fabrics and trace around them.
5. Cut out each piece, adding approximately ³⁄₁₆" allowance around the outer edges.
6. Place each appliqué piece on the background, following your positioning lines, and pin. Refer to the appliqué order as you place each piece.

Stitching the Pieces in Place

We prefer the needle-turn appliqué technique.
1. Start with a single strand of thread approximately 18" long. Tie a knot in one end.
2. Start stitching on a relatively straight edge and turn under the seam allowance as you stitch.

Use the thumb and index finger of your other hand like a clamp, holding the turned seam allowance down on the background. Use the blind stitch to sew the edges of the appliqué to the background.

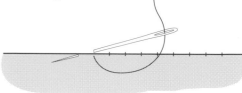

3. Clip the seam allowances at inside corners and on inside curves.

4. For sharp points and outside corners, stitch all the way to the tip of the point before turning under the seam allowances on the other side.

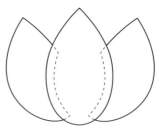

5. If an edge of one appliqué piece will be covered by another, it is not necessary to turn under the edge that will be covered. This avoids bulk.

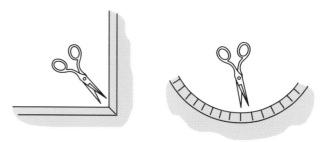

Appliqué side petals before central petal.

6. If a dark-colored background "shadows" or shows through the appliquéd pieces, cut it away from the back of the completed appliqué, leaving a ¼" allowance of the background all around.

7. When the appliqué is complete, remove any markings that remain exposed on the surface of the quilt. Press the top, right side down, on a towel to prevent "shine" and to maintain the relief.

Making Flower Stems

Bias bars are a handy tool for making the narrow stems that curve gracefully in many appliqué designs. These flat metal or nylon rods are available in varying widths; ⅛"- to ½"-wide bars are the most commonly used sizes.

1. Cut bias strips of fabric twice the desired finished width plus ½" for seam allowances. For example, if you want the finished stem to be ⅜" wide, cut the bias strip 1¼" wide.

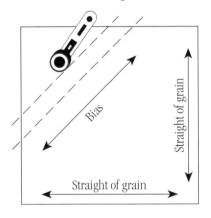

2. Fold the bias strip in half lengthwise with *wrong sides together*. Stitch so that when you measure from the fold, the distance from the fold to the stitching is slightly wider than the finished stem width—just enough so you can slip the bias bar inside the resulting tube.

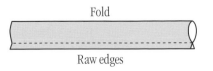

Fold

Raw edges

3. Trim the seam allowance to ¼" (narrower if your finished stem will be narrower). Slip the bias bar into the fabric tube and position the seam so it is in the center of the flat portion of the bar. Steam press the tube flat with the seam allowance to one side.

4. Carefully remove the bias bar. *It may be quite hot!* Position the stem on the background fabric and pin in place. Appliqué the edge of the inside curve first before you do the outside curve.

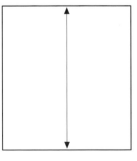

Adding Borders

Most quilt tops require a border to contain the design and draw the eye into the quilt. We prefer to use the lengthwise grain for borders. For information on choosing border fabrics for your quilt, refer to "Finishing Up" on pages 95–100.

You may attach borders with either straight-cut corners or mitered corners. Directions for both types of border applications follow.

Straight-Cut Corners

1. To prevent the edges of the quilt from rippling and ruffling, measure lengthwise through the center of the quilt top, *not along the raw edges*. Measure from the top edge to the bottom edge for the length to cut the side border strips.

Quiltmaking Basics ❧ 105

2. Cut two border strips of the desired width to match this length. Fold each border strip in half and place a pin at the center. Establish the center point of each half of the strip and mark with a pin so the border strip is divided into quarters. Repeat this marking process along the raw edge of the pieced quilt top.

3. Pin the border strip to the quilt top, matching the marking pins and easing to fit as necessary. Stitch, using a ¼"-wide seam allowance.
4. For the top and bottom borders, measure the quilt top across the center, including the side borders. Cut two border strips to this length and attach to the quilt top as described for the side borders in steps 2 and 3.

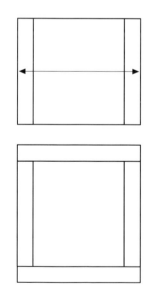

Mitered Corners
1. Estimate the outside dimensions (length and width) of the completed quilt with borders and add 3" to each measurement (for safety's sake). Cut border strips to these lengths. If you want to attach multiple borders to your quilt top, cut the required strips from each border fabric

and sew them together to each side of the quilt. That way, you can attach them for each side of the quilt as one border.
2. To determine the finished size of the quilt top, measure the quilt top through the center and record the length minus ½" for seam allowances, and the width minus ½" for seam allowances.

Length - ½" = _____
Width - ½" = _____

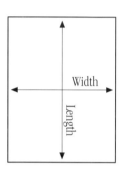

3. Find the center of each border strip and mark this point with a pin. Measure away from this point in both directions, a distance that is half the length for the lengthwise borders and half the width for the crosswise borders. Place pins at these points. Establish the center point of each half of the strip and mark with a pin so the border strip is divided into quarters. Place pins at these points.
4. Find the center of each side of the pieced quilt top and mark with a pin. Measure ¼" in from the outer edge of each corner and mark with a pin. When attaching the borders, start or stop stitching at this point. Establish and pin the quarter marks on the quilt top as you did on the border strips.

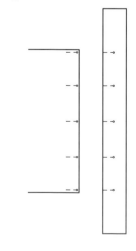

5. Pin the borders to the quilt top, matching pins and easing as necessary. Stitch, using a ¼"-wide seam allowance. Remember to start and stop stitching ¼" in from each corner of the quilt top.

6. Miter one corner at a time. Spread a corner of the quilt smooth and straight on the pressing area, with the excess border strips extending from Side A to overlap the excess border of Side B. Make sure that the two borders are at a 90° angle to each other.

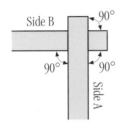

7. Fold under the top excess border fabric of Side A at a 45° angle. Make sure that the top and bottom edges of the border strip extensions are exactly even. When you are sure that the corner is square and the resulting angle is 45°, press the fold flat. This fold line is the sewing line for the mitered corner. Pin to secure.

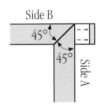

8. Flip the border of Side A up to match the raw edge of Side B so the quilt is folded on the diagonal, exposing the wrong side. Pin across the fold to secure. Stitch along the fold from the outside edge of the border toward the pieced center. Stop stitching when you are ¼" away from the innermost edge of the border. Trim the excess border ¼" from stitching. Press well. Repeat with the remaining corners.

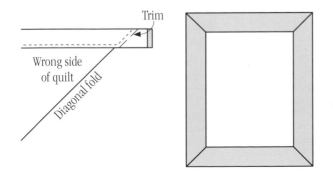

Quilting

Quilting stitches hold the three quilt-sandwich layers (top, batting, and backing) together and prevent the batting from shifting. Before you can quilt, however, you must choose a design, prepare the backing, and choose a batting. After basting the layers together, you are ready to quilt by hand or machine.

Marking the Design

Refer to "Finishing Up" on pages 95–100 for quilting design ideas for your quilt. After selecting your quilting design, mark it on the quilt top before basting the layers together. Take care and use caution when selecting your marking tool. Always test any marking tool on sample fabrics used in your quilt to make sure the lines can be easily removed by washing.

If you plan to machine quilt using straight lines, gentle curves, and/or free-motion designs, it may not be necessary to mark the quilting design on the quilt top.

Preparing the Backing

For best results, the backing should be the same fiber content as the front. We use 100% cotton and preshrink it. Review pages 96–97 for additional information on selecting fabrics for backing your quilt.

Make the backing at least 2" larger than the top on all sides. If it is necessary to piece the backing to make it wide enough or long enough, use three panels rather than two for a more pleasing appearance and to avoid a center seam. Trim off selvages and press the seam allowances open.

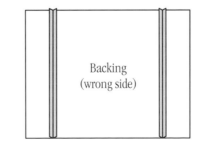

Selecting the Batting

Batting is the filler layer between the top and the backing of the quilt. Consider the fiber content and loft (thickness) of the batting when making your selection. Since most Round Robin projects become wall hangings rather than bed quilts, a low-loft or thin batting is most desirable.

Batting fiber content is a matter of personal choice. The 100% polyester batts are usually bonded to keep the fibers from shifting and they are very stable. Less quilting is needed to hold the quilt layers together. Polyester batting is easy to handle for both machine and hand quilting. However, the fibers of some polyester battings migrate to the surface of the quilt and create tiny "beards" or "pills."

Some of the older all-cotton battings required very closely spaced quilting to prevent the layers from shifting and separating during laundering. Some of the new 100% cotton battings are low-loft and do not require such closely spaced quilting. Also, cotton battings do not beard.

Cotton flannel can also be used as a quilt batting. It must be prewashed and dried (several times if possible) since flannel tends to shrink more than the cotton fabrics in your quilt top. Because flannel is woven, you can space the quilting lines quite far apart. Quilts made with flannel batting are lightweight and have a flat look.

Cotton/polyester (80%/20%) battings are also low-loft. The cotton content reduces the chances of bearding, and the polyester bonds the fibers together. That means the quilting lines can be spaced farther apart (every 2" to 3").

It is extremely important to follow the manufacturer's directions for soaking or washing battings that contain cotton. They need to be preshrunk as much as possible before using them.

Polyester battings are easy for both hand and machine quilters to "needle." If you plan to machine quilt, pin-baste the layers more closely as polyester is more slippery than cotton. Cotton battings are wonderful for machine quilting because the fibers of the batting adhere to the top and backing fabrics. This helps prevent the shifting and stretching that causes distortion when you use a polyester batting. If you plan to hand quilt, experiment with stitching on a sample of cotton batting. Some of them are difficult to "needle."

Pretreat batting as recommended by the manufacturer. Let all battings lie on a flat surface for a day or so before using to allow them to expand and take a big breath of fresh air after being stuffed into that tiny plastic bag. Cut the batting at least 2" larger than the quilt top on all sides.

Basting the Quilt Layers Together

We recommend thread basting the quilt layers together if you plan to hand quilt. You may use safety pins or extra-long straight pins to baste for machine quilting.

Basting for Hand Quilting

1. Cut the backing and batting at least 2" larger than the quilt top on each side.
2. Lay the backing fabric, wrong side up, on a large, flat surface. Working from the center out, smooth out all wrinkles and either tape or pin the edges to the work surface, pulling the backing gently taut but not stretched.
3. Place the batting in the center of the backing and smooth it out from the center to eliminate any wrinkles.
4. Place the quilt top, right side up, in the center of the batting. Starting from the center, smooth it out so it is completely flat and wrinkle-free. Pin the edges to the batting and backing.
5. Working from the center out, pin-baste the three layers together. Smooth any fullness toward the edges, adjusting pins at the outer edge if necessary.
6. Using a large needle threaded with white thread, baste the layers together diagonally, vertically, and horizontally. Space the basting rows 6" apart and remove the pins as you go. Baste around the outer edges of the quilt.

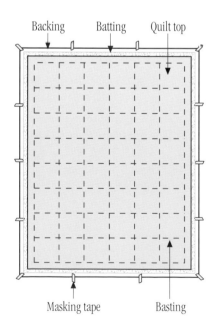

Backing   Batting   Quilt top

Masking tape   Basting

Basting for Machine Quilting

Substitute pin basting for hand basting if you plan to machine quilt. Basting threads get caught in the foot of the machine while you are quilting. The layers tend to roll together and shift, causing stretching and distortion. In addition, it is difficult to remove basting threads when you have made quilting stitches over them.

Take time to do a good job of pin basting. Layers that are well pinned are much easier to quilt. Careful pin basting helps prevent distortion and stretching during stitching and eliminates unwanted tucks and puckers on both sides of the quilt.

1. Fold the top of the quilt in half lengthwise and mark the center of the top and bottom edges with a pin. Mark the backing fabric and batting in the same manner. Measure the quilt top along the fold, from edge to edge, for the lengthwise measurement.

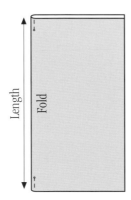

2. Working on a flat surface or table at least 3 feet by 5 feet, mark the center of the tabletop surface on one of the short sides. Use a toothpick secured by masking tape to make the mark. This makes a center "bump" you can feel when centering the layers. Measure down the length of the surface from the marked center point until you reach the lengthwise

measurement of the quilt top plus 3". Place another toothpick secured by masking tape on the table to mark this point. If the measurement is longer than the table, mark the center of its edge.

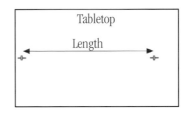

3. Fold the backing fabric in half lengthwise, wrong sides together. Place on the table, matching the center marks of the backing with the toothpicks.

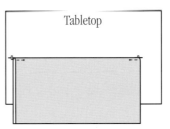

4. Unfold the backing with wrong side up, allowing the excess to hang over the table edges if necessary. Check to make sure the centers are still aligned by feeling the toothpick bumps. Carefully smooth the fabric open. Use binder clamps to gently stretch and securely hold the backing to one side of the table. Then attach more binder clamps to the opposite side of the table. If your backing is long enough to reach the edges of the table, apply binder clamps to the remaining two sides. If not, apply several pieces of masking tape to the unclamped backing edges to secure it to the table. The backing fabric should now be taut but not stretched or distorted.

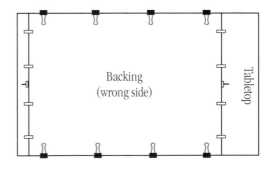

5. Fold the batting in half lengthwise and gently place it on top of the backing, making sure the center of the batting matches the toothpick bumps. Unfold it and carefully smooth it out so there are no bumps or wrinkles. Do not clamp to the table.

6. Fold the quilt top in half lengthwise, right sides together, and place it on top of the batting and backing. Match the center of the quilt top with the toothpick bumps. Unfold it and carefully smooth the top. The sandwich is ready for pin basting.

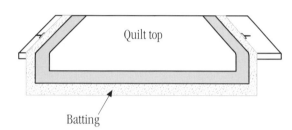

Quilt top

Batting

7. Pin the layers together using #1, nickel-plated safety pins or extra-long straight pins. The safety pins take more time to clasp and unclasp but are very secure. Straight pins take less time to position but are not as secure and sometimes inflict pain while you are working. Some quilters prefer to use a combination of pins, using the safety pins where extra security is needed and straight pins in areas that will be quilted first. Begin pinning in the center, working toward the outside edges, pinning every 2" to 3". Be careful not to scratch the surface of the table.

If your quilt is larger than the table, remove the clamps and adjust the layers so a new section is on the tabletop, ready to pin. Reclamp the backing to the table on the unpinned side only. Continue until the entire surface is adequately pinned.

Hand Quilting

Many quilters enjoy methodically touching and savoring all their fabrics in the quilt one last time by hand quilting. For hand quilting, use a thread with the same fiber content as the fabrics in your quilt. We recommend 100% cotton. Quilting needles are referred to as "betweens." The higher the size number, the finer and shorter the needle. Size 12 is the smallest. Most hand quilters strive to use a size 12 between needle because the shorter and finer the needle, the shorter and more closely spaced the stitches will be. Beginners may find it easier to start with a size 9 or 10 and then work up to size 12. At first, concentrate on even stitches rather than the length. The ability to make short quilting stitches develops with practice.

Most quilters use a frame or hoop to support the quilt area in which they are working and to keep it smooth. A thimble is a must for the center finger of your quilting hand. Find one that is comfortable—not too snug and not too loose.

To hand quilt:
1. Thread the needle with approximately an 18" length of thread and knot one end. Longer lengths tend to tangle.

2. Always start quilting in the center of the quilt and work your way out to the edges. Begin by inserting the needle through the top layer and batting only, about 1" away from where you want to begin your stitching line. Then bring the needle back out at the starting point. Give the thread a quick tug so the knot will pop into the batting— hidden forever.

3. Start with a small backstitch. Continue stitching, using a "rocking motion." Set the eye end of the needle in a groove of the thimble and guide the fabric in front of the needle with the thumb of the same hand. Place the index or middle finger of your other hand under the quilt. Make a small running stitch through all the layers.

4. When you are near the end of the thread or have finished the line of stitching, make a small knot close to the last stitch. To do this, wind

the thread around the needle three or four times and pull the needle through these windings until a knot forms.

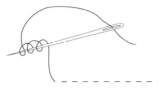

5. Make one small backstitch and take a quick tug to bury the knot. Clip the thread tails at the surface of the quilt.

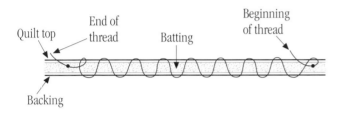

Machine Quilting

Your sewing machine must be in good working order for machine quilting. Good lighting is also very important. Position a table on the left side and one at the back of the machine to help support the weight of a medium-to-large quilt as you feed it through the sewing machine.

There are several options when it comes to choosing thread for the top of the quilt. You can use 100% cotton thread, size 50, 3-ply, in a color that matches the fabric. If there is a variety of fabrics, you can use invisible, monofilament nylon thread to blend the colors. Use clear, invisible thread in the light areas and smoke-colored invisible thread in the darker areas of the quilt top. You can also use variegated rayon thread in the same manner.

In the bobbin, use 100% cotton thread, size 50, 3-ply, in a color that matches the backing fabric. Wind several bobbins before you begin stitching to eliminate the frustration of stopping to wind bobbins after you start quilting.

When your machine is threaded correctly, check the stitches for balanced tension and make any necessary adjustments before quilting.

There are several methods of tying knots or securing the beginning and ending stitches. Donna uses a technique based on the fact that short stitches sewn closely together are diffi-

cult to remove. (Just try to take them out when you are doing regular sewing!) Set your machine for a short stitch length (.5/inch for European model machines or 20 stitches/inch for American models). Take 4 to 5 stitches at this setting when you begin a line of quilting stitches. Lengthen the stitch slightly (1.0 or 18 stitches/inch) and take 4 to 5 more stitches. Continue in this fashion until the setting is at 3.0 or 10 stitches/inch (or a stitch length that is pleasing to you) and then continue quilting. This method of securing the stitches should happen within the first and last inch of your line of stitching. (Reverse the process at the end of the line by gradually decreasing the stitch length until it is .5 or 20 stitches/inch.)

There are two basic types of machine quilting. The first method is used for machine quilting straight lines or gentle curves. Use a walking foot or even-feed foot for tuck-free and pucker-free, straight-line machine quilting.

The second type of machine quilting is used when you wish to do elaborate curves and free-motion quilting lines, for example, quilting around motifs or allover stipple quilting. Set your machine for darning, referring to your machine manual for directions and attach the darning presser foot. Use your hands to control the movement of the fabric as you stitch. Practice stitching, working to achieve a smooth and even rhythm as you learn to coordinate your hands and the movement of the fabric with the speed of the machine to create nice, even stitches.

When machine quilting, the quilt top occasionally "creeps" a little, and it may be necessary to use more pins in areas where excess fabric seems to appear.

When machine quilting, do not begin in the center and move out to the edges as in hand quilting. Instead, first secure the layers and divide the top into manageable sections. This helps eliminate shifting and distortion while you complete the remainder of the quilting.

To machine quilt Border Beauties quilts:

1. Using the walking foot, stitch in-the-ditch as close to the inside of each border as possible to secure the layers for additional quilting. For example, in-the-ditch quilting is done in every straight, lengthwise, and vertical seam of each round in "There's a Cat Loose in My Sewing Room."

2. Add more quilting to enhance the beauty of each border of your quilt. For straight lines or gentle curves, use the walking foot. If your quilting design calls for more intricate, curved lines, such as outlining motifs or stipple quilting, set your sewing machine for darning and use the free-motion method of machine quilting. Barbara used the walking foot to quilt along the outer edge of each musical staff in the outer border of "There's a Cat Loose in My Sewing Room," as well as around the cat and the sewing tools. (She hand quilted around the appliquéd garland with hearts as well as in the central Basket block, although these areas could have been machine quilted as well.)

To machine quilt Add-On Appliqué quilts:

1. Using the walking foot, stitch-in-the ditch on the quilt top as close to the inside of the border(s) as possible.

2. Secure the entire quilt top to help prevent shifting and distortion by outlining some of the motifs. Select appliquéd pieces that are approximately 10" to 12" apart. Use the walking foot method to outline motifs that have straight lines and gentle curves. Use the darning foot, free-motion method for machine quilting around motifs with intricate, curved lines.

3. After securing the layers, quilt around the remaining motifs and use design lines to add highlights. Fill in the background to bring out the beauty of the quilt theme by using stipple, echo, or random quilting lines, or other design of your choice.

To machine quilt Around-the-Block quilts:

1. Using the walking foot, stitch-in-the ditch on the quilt top as close to the inside of the border(s) as possible.

2. Stitch in-the-ditch around the theme block.

3. Stitch through the center lines of the quilt, both vertically and horizontally, or as close to the center lines as possible. Sew additional vertical and horizontal lines as needed to make sections approximately 12" square. It is OK to interrupt a stitching line to avoid stitching across a motif.

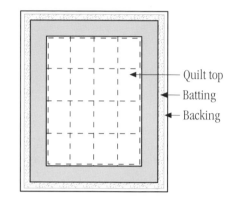

— Quilt top
— Batting
— Backing

4. Add more quilting design lines to enhance the theme of the quilt. For straight lines or gentle curves, use the walking foot. As you quilt, be aware of the "section lines" you have already stitched and be careful when crossing them so that tucks and puckers do not form. Use extra pins as needed to gently ease in any extra fullness. Use free-motion machine-quilting techniques to outline motifs, add highlights, and fill in the background.

Binding Your Quilt

When the quilting is completed, you are ready to bind the edges of your quilt. First, remove all basting, pins, and markings. Using a rotary cutter and ruler, trim away excess backing and batting. Make sure corners are square. Be sure the batting extends evenly to the outer edges of the quilt. Then cut binding strips on the straight grain or the bias after determining the desired width. We prefer double-fold French binding.

A double-fold French binding cut on the straight or bias grain is a neat and very durable finish for the edges of your quilt. If the quilt has curved or scalloped edges, you must cut the binding strips on the bias.

For double-fold binding, cut strips six times the desired width plus ¼". The extra ¼" is for the fabric that will be lost in the turn of the folds.

For example, if you want a finished binding ⅜" wide, cut the binding strips 2½" wide (⅜" x 6 = 2¼" + ¼" = 2½").

Calculate the amount of binding you will need to go around the finished quilt top and add an extra 20" for turning corners and for security and peace of mind. For example, if the quilt top measures 24" x 42", you will need 152" of binding (42" + 24" + 42" + 24" + 20" = 152").

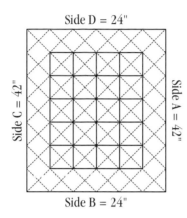

Side D = 24"
Side C = 42"
Side A = 42"
Side B = 24"

Straight-of-Grain Binding

1. After figuring the required amount of binding, cut strips from the crosswise grain of the fabric. One cut across the crosswise grain will give you approximately 40" of binding.
2. Sew the strips together at a 45° angle and press seams open.

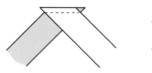

Cut strip ends at a 45° angle and seam.

Press seams open.

3. Fold the strip in half lengthwise, wrong sides together, and press.

Bias Binding

1. Cut bias binding from a square of fabric. To determine the size of the square needed, multiply the total amount of binding needed by the cut width of the bias strip you plan to use. Total Binding Needed x Cut Bias Strip Width = X. Using a calculator, find the square root of X. The resulting number will be the size of the beginning square.

For example, for a 24" x 42" quilt requiring 152" of double-fold bias-cut binding that finishes to ½", you will cut bias strips 3¼" wide. (½" x 6 = 3" + ¼" = 3¼"). To determine the size of the beginning square, multiply 152" x 3¼" = 494. The square root of 494 is 22.2. Rounding this figure up to the nearest inch means you will need to start with a 23" fabric square.

2. Cut the required square of binding fabric and pin-mark the center of the square at the top and bottom edges. Cut the square in half on the diagonal to yield two large half-square triangles.

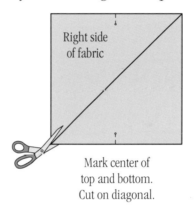

Right side of fabric

Mark center of top and bottom. Cut on diagonal.

3. Place the right sides together so the pin-marked edges align. The ¼" tails will be exposed at each end, and the center pins will not match. Sew the pin-marked edges together with a ¼"-wide seam. Press the seam open.

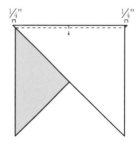

¼"   ¼"

4. Measuring from bias side A, line up your ruler at the width required for the cut bias strips. Using your rotary cutter, make a cut approximately 3" long. Be sure the cut is parallel to side A.

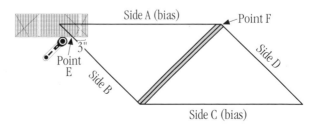

Side A (bias)
Point F
Point E
3"
Side B
Side D
Side C (bias)

5. With right sides together, pull side B around to meet side D. Match point E to point F and pin the raw edges together.

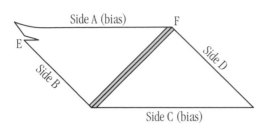

Side A (bias)
F
E
Side B
Side D
Side C (bias)

6. Stitch ¼" from the raw edges and press the seam open. You will have a tube with a free-hanging, 3"-long tail at one end and an extension on the other end.

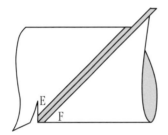

E
F

7. Place a rotary-cutting mat on your ironing board and slip the tube around the end of the ironing board, being careful not to stretch it. Cut a continuous bias strip from the tube as shown.

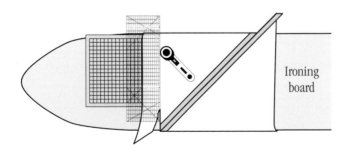

Ironing board

8. Fold the binding strip in half lengthwise, wrong sides together, and press.

Binding Application

1. Beginning near an inconspicuous corner on one edge of the quilt, pin the binding to the front side of the quilt, with the raw edge at the end of the binding folded at a 45° angle.

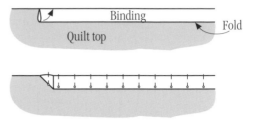

Binding
Quilt top
Fold

2. Use an even-feed foot, if available, to sew the binding to the quilt. Make the seam allowance the same as the finished width of the binding. For example, if the finished width of the binding is ½", then you will stitch the binding to the quilt using a ½"-wide seam allowance. Be careful not to stretch the binding or the quilt top as you sew. When approaching a corner, stop stitching the width of a seam allowance from the corner. Backstitch. For example, if your finished binding is to be ½" wide, stop stitching ½" from the corner; backstitch and clip the threads.

3. Turn the quilt. Fold the binding straight up and away from the quilt to form a 45°-angle fold.

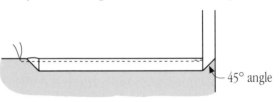

45° angle

4. Hold the fold down with your finger and bring the binding straight down along the edge of the quilt. There will be a fold in the binding that should align with the first side. Pin. Beginning at the top of the fold in the binding, stitch. This creates a mitered fold in the binding at the corner of the quilt.

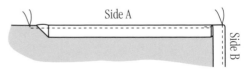

Side A
Side B

5. Continue sewing and mitering corners around the remaining edges of the quilt. When you reach the starting point, overlap the beginning of the binding ½" beyond the beginning stitches; backstitch and clip the threads.

6. Fold the binding over the raw edges to the back of the quilt and place the folded edge of the binding so that it hides the machine stitching line. Blindstitch in place, making sure stitches do not show on the front or back.

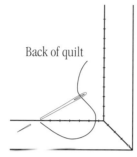

Back of quilt

7. At the corners, a perfect miter will form on the front of the quilt. Form a miter on the back by folding it in the opposite direction from the miter on the top side of the quilt; this distributes the bulk of the fabric evenly. Stitch the miters closed on both sides of the quilt.

Adding a Hanging Sleeve

Round Robin quilts are most often displayed on the wall and require a sleeve at the top of the backing for easy hanging. For the least noticeable sleeve, use a piece of the backing fabric or select one that goes well with the front and the backing.

1. To make a 4"-wide sleeve (finished size), cut a strip of fabric 8½" wide and as long as the top edge of the quilt. Turn under ½" at each short end of the strip and press. Turn under an additional ½", press, and stitch in place close to the fold.

2. Fold the strip in half lengthwise, right side out. Pin and stitch ¼" from the raw edge to make a long tube.

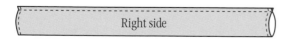

Right side

3. Center the seam on one side of the tube. Press the seam open and the tube flat.

4. Position the sleeve at the top edge on the back of the quilt just below the binding. Hand stitch all four sides of the sleeve to the back of the quilt, making sure the stitches do not go through to the front of the quilt. Be sure to leave the tube open at both ends.

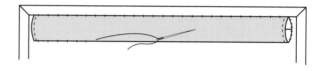

5. Purchase a straight (not warped) piece of lath from a building-supply store. Cut it slightly shorter than the width of the top edge of the quilt and drill a hole near each end of the board. Position the lath on the wall where you wish to hang the quilt and mark the nail positions through the holes. Hammer nails into the wall and hang your masterpiece.

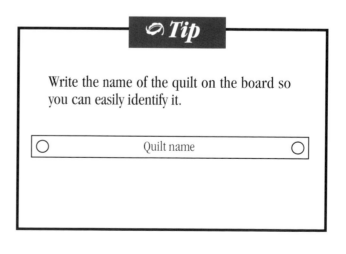

✑ Tip

Write the name of the quilt on the board so you can easily identify it.

Quilt name

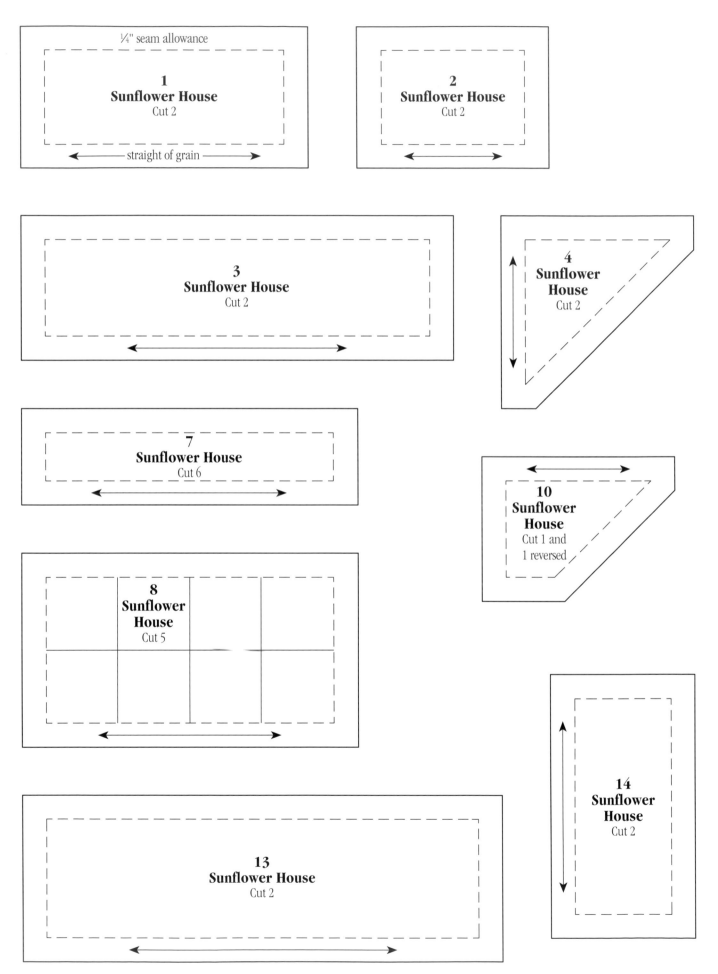

¼" seam allowance

1
Sunflower House
Cut 2

← straight of grain →

2
Sunflower House
Cut 2

3
Sunflower House
Cut 2

4
Sunflower House
Cut 2

7
Sunflower House
Cut 6

10
Sunflower House
Cut 1 and
1 reversed

8
Sunflower House
Cut 5

13
Sunflower House
Cut 2

14
Sunflower House
Cut 2

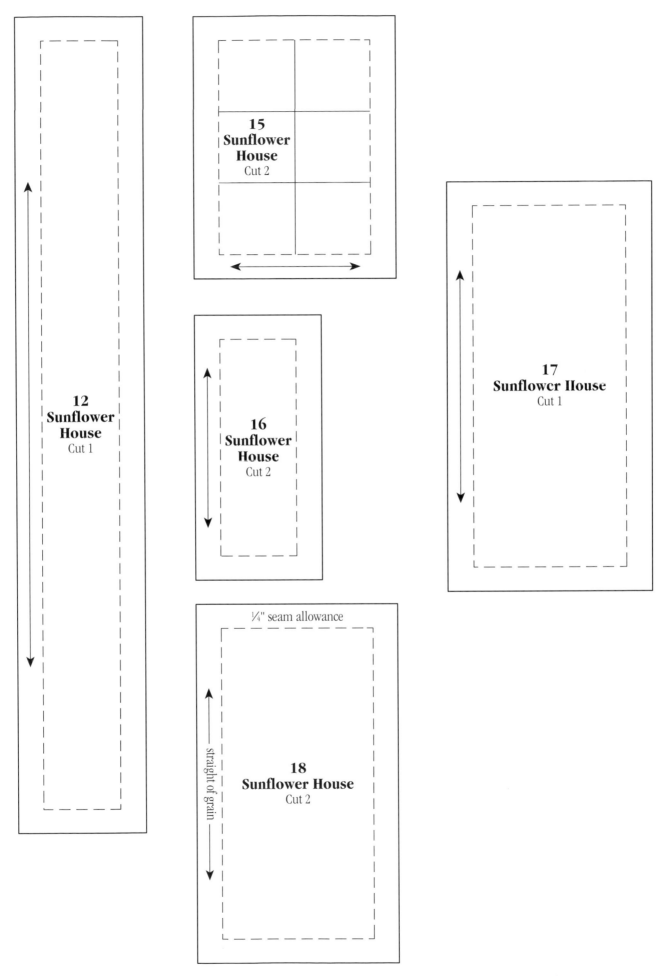

15
Sunflower
House
Cut 2

12
Sunflower
House
Cut 1

16
Sunflower
House
Cut 2

17
Sunflower House
Cut 1

¼" seam allowance

straight of grain

18
Sunflower House
Cut 2

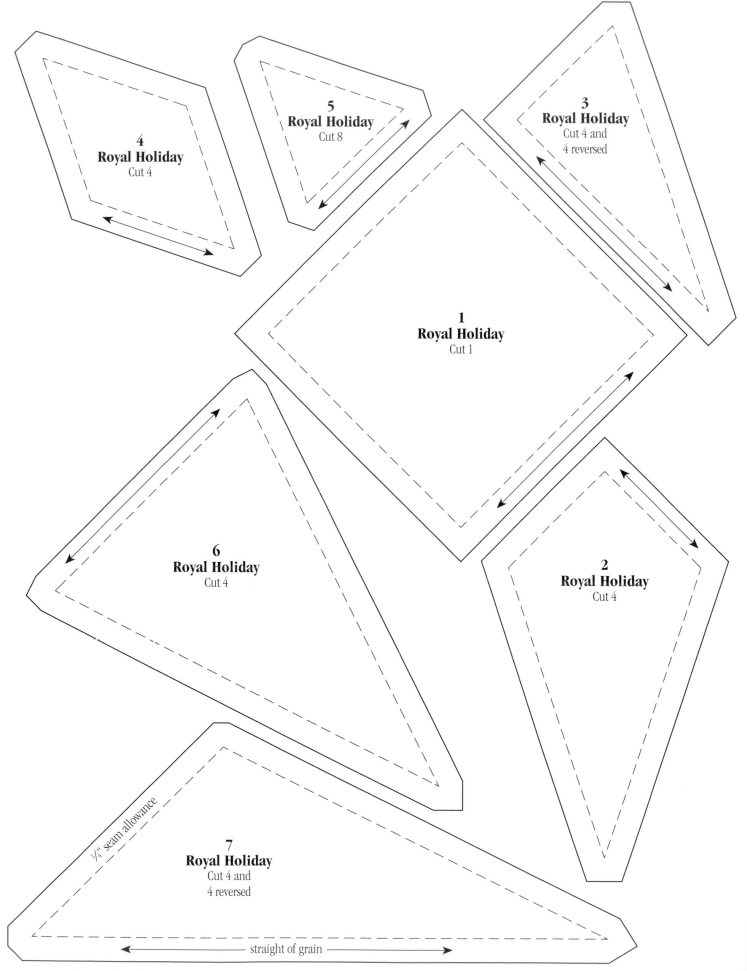

4
Royal Holiday
Cut 4

5
Royal Holiday
Cut 8

3
Royal Holiday
Cut 4 and
4 reversed

1
Royal Holiday
Cut 1

6
Royal Holiday
Cut 4

2
Royal Holiday
Cut 4

¼" seam allowance

7
Royal Holiday
Cut 4 and
4 reversed

straight of grain

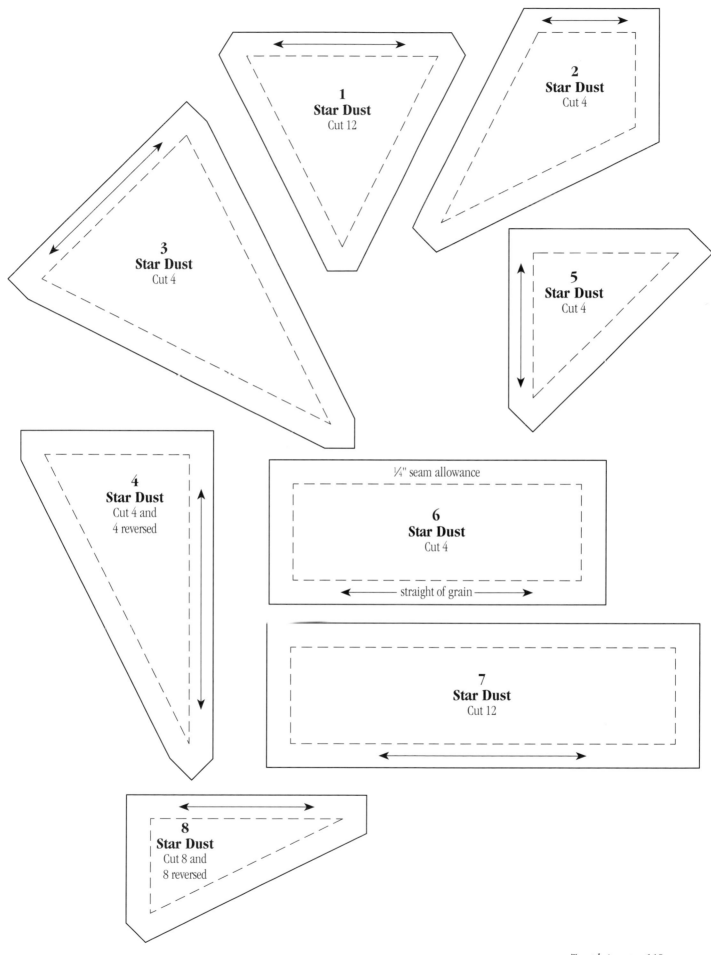

1
Star Dust
Cut 12

2
Star Dust
Cut 4

3
Star Dust
Cut 4

5
Star Dust
Cut 4

4
Star Dust
Cut 4 and
4 reversed

¼" seam allowance

6
Star Dust
Cut 4

straight of grain

7
Star Dust
Cut 12

8
Star Dust
Cut 8 and
8 reversed

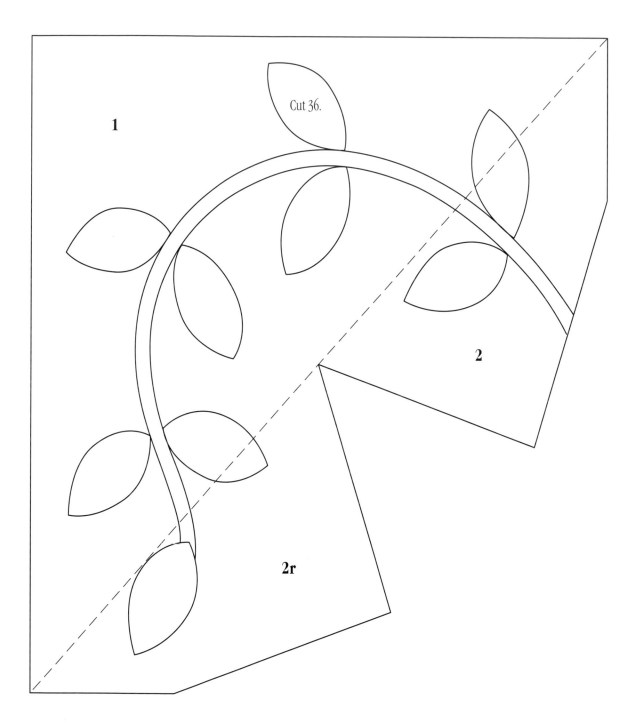

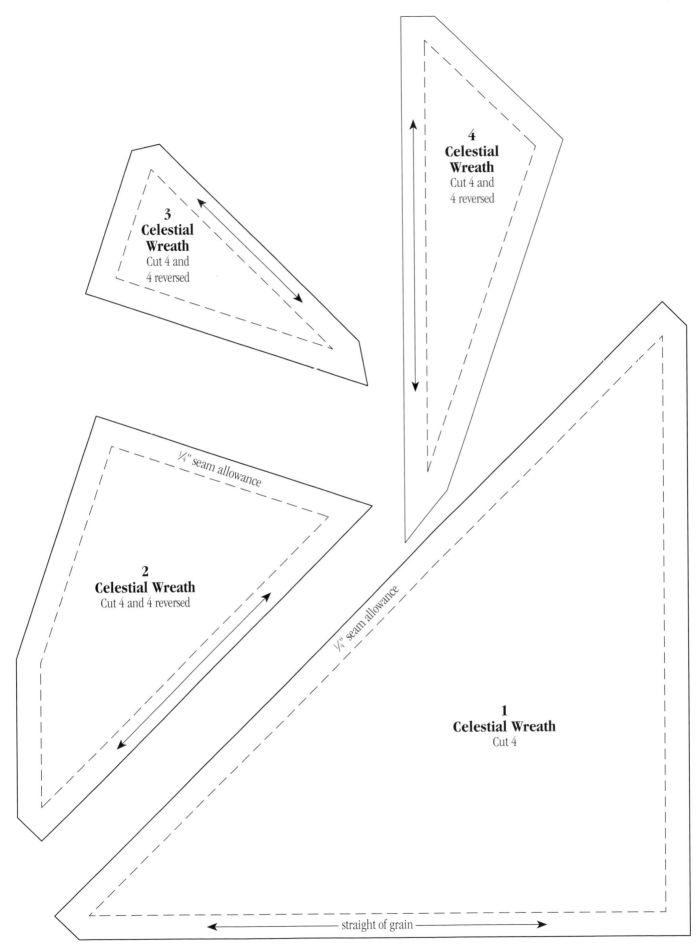

3
Celestial
Wreath
Cut 4 and
4 reversed

4
Celestial
Wreath
Cut 4 and
4 reversed

¼" seam allowance

2
Celestial Wreath
Cut 4 and 4 reversed

¼" seam allowance

1
Celestial Wreath
Cut 4

straight of grain

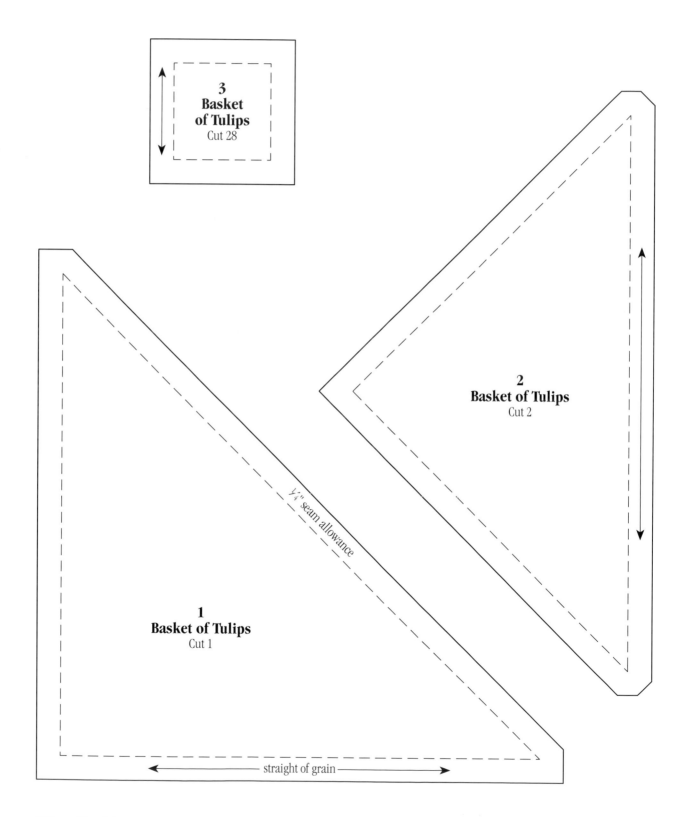

3
**Basket
of Tulips**
Cut 28

2
Basket of Tulips
Cut 2

¼" seam allowance

1
Basket of Tulips
Cut 1

straight of grain

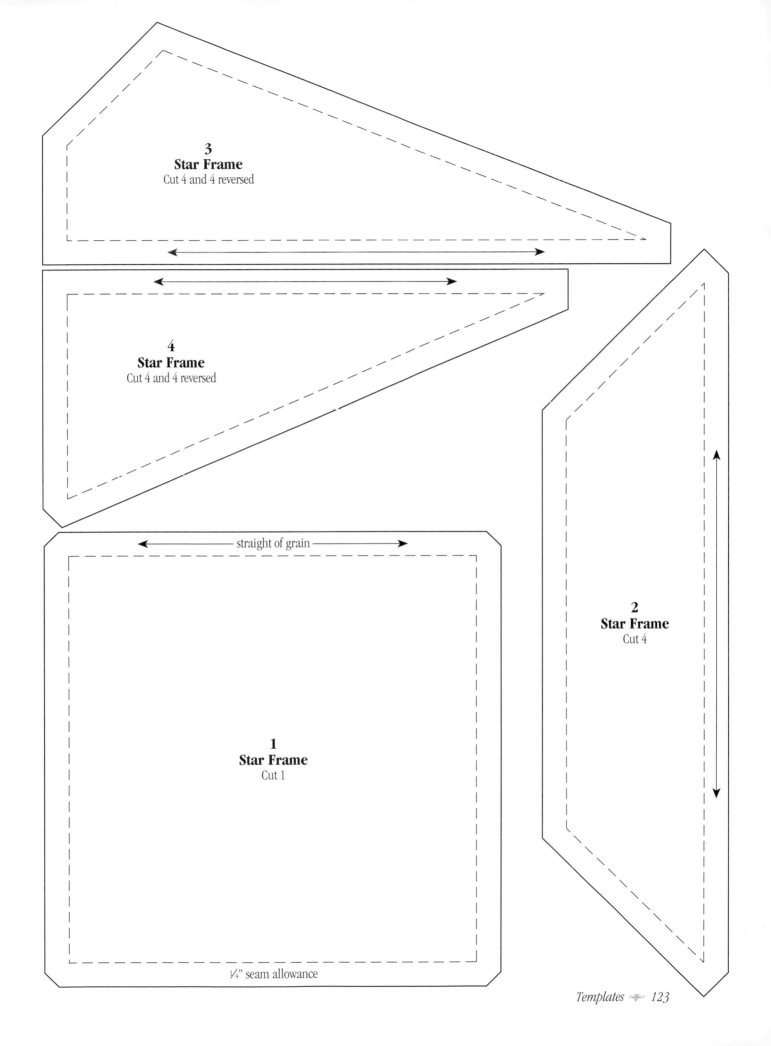

3
Star Frame
Cut 4 and 4 reversed

4
Star Frame
Cut 4 and 4 reversed

2
Star Frame
Cut 4

straight of grain

1
Star Frame
Cut 1

¼" seam allowance

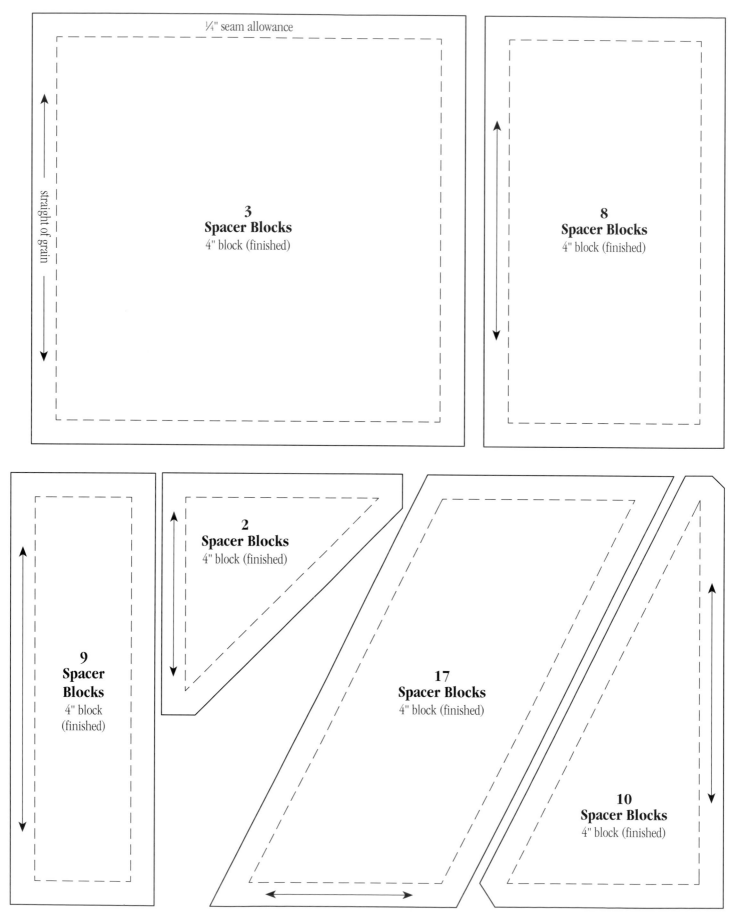

¼" seam allowance

straight of grain

3
Spacer Blocks
4" block (finished)

8
Spacer Blocks
4" block (finished)

9
Spacer
Blocks
4" block
(finished)

2
Spacer Blocks
4" block (finished)

17
Spacer Blocks
4" block (finished)

10
Spacer Blocks
4" block (finished)

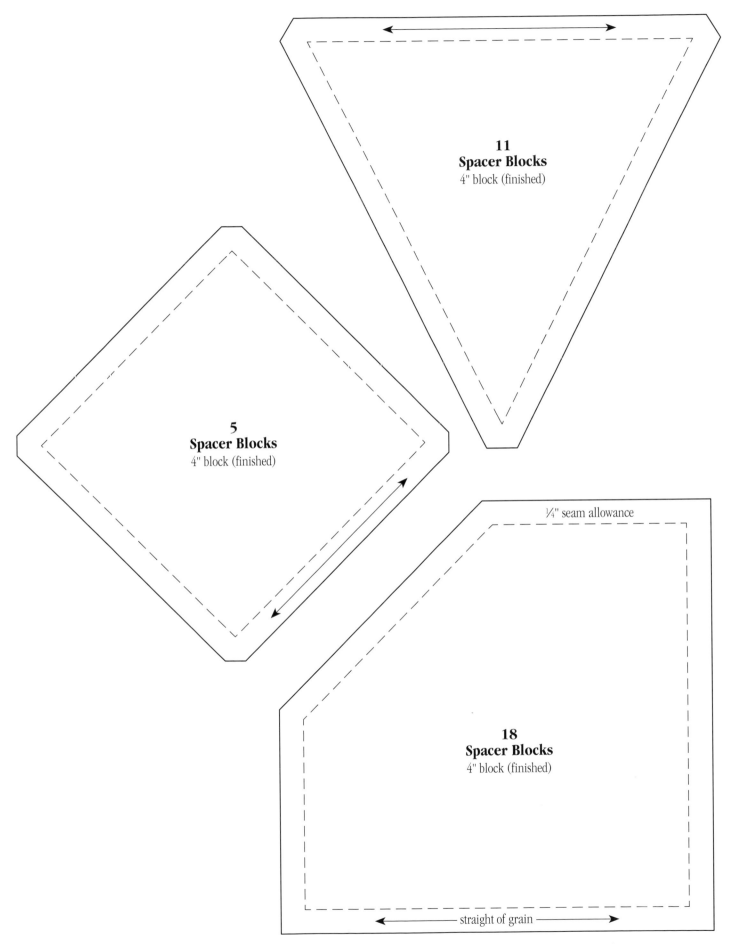

11
Spacer Blocks
4" block (finished)

5
Spacer Blocks
4" block (finished)

¼" seam allowance

18
Spacer Blocks
4" block (finished)

straight of grain

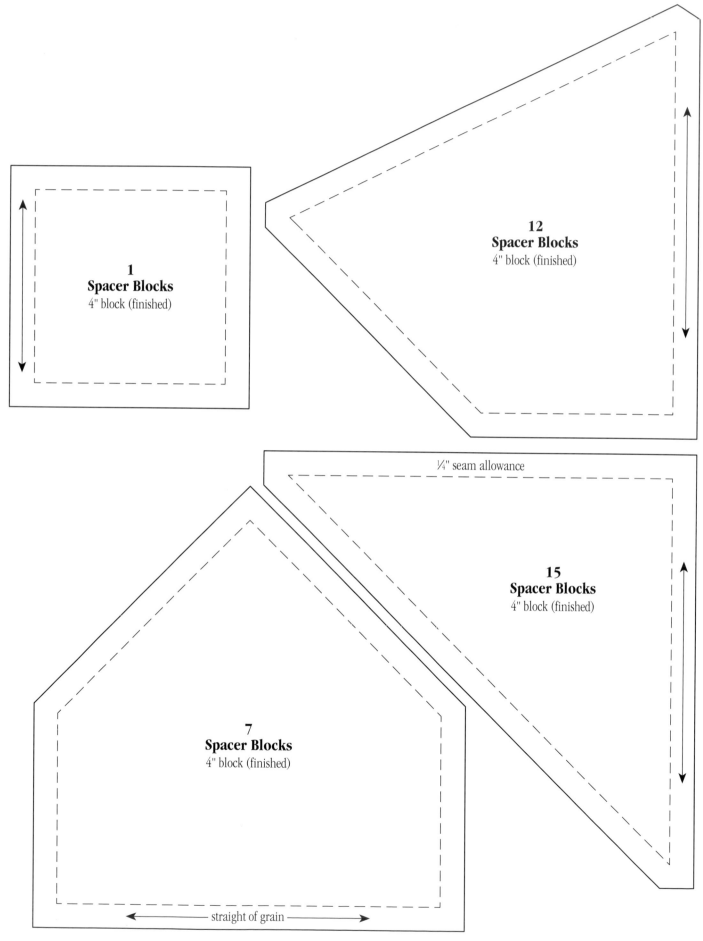

1
Spacer Blocks
4" block (finished)

12
Spacer Blocks
4" block (finished)

¼" seam allowance

15
Spacer Blocks
4" block (finished)

7
Spacer Blocks
4" block (finished)

straight of grain

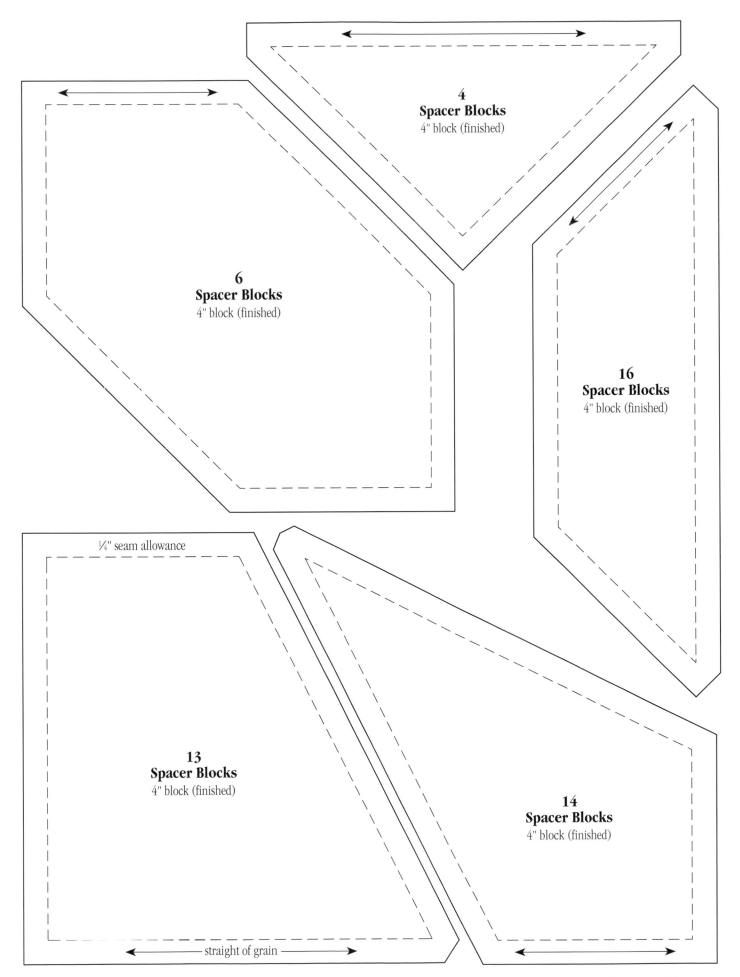

4
Spacer Blocks
4" block (finished)

6
Spacer Blocks
4" block (finished)

16
Spacer Blocks
4" block (finished)

¼" seam allowance

13
Spacer Blocks
4" block (finished)

14
Spacer Blocks
4" block (finished)

straight of grain

Templates ❦ *127*

Bibliography

Beyer, Jinny. *Medallion Quilts*. McLean, Va.: EPM Publications, Inc., 1982. A comprehensive source for medallion design.

———. *The Quilter's Album of Blocks and Borders*. McLean, Va.: EPM Publications, Inc., 1986. This reference book features a variety of blocks and borders.

Herberholz, Donald and Barbara Herberholz. *Art Works for Elementary Teachers*. Dubuque, Iowa: Wm C. Brown Publishers, 1990. A good basic book on design.

Hopkins, Judy. *One-of-a-Kind Quilts*. Bothell, Wash.: That Patchwork Place, Inc., 1989. The quilter who wants to explore designing on the grid system will find a wealth of knowledge here.

Kimball, Jeana. *Reflections of Baltimore*. Bothell, Wash.: That Patchwork Place, Inc., 1989. An extensive source on hand-appliqué techniques.

Lauer, David A. *Design Basics*. Austin, Texas: Holt, Rinehart, Winston, Inc., 1990. An excellent reference on art design and composition.

Liby, Shirley. *Borders, Borders, Borders*. Muncie, Ind.: Royal Printing, 1990. Contains many illustrations of borders.

Marston, Gwen, and Joe Cunningham. *Sets and Borders*. Paducah, Ky: American Quilters Society, 1987. Good text and illustrations for planning and designing borders.

Nadelstern, Paula and LynNell Hancock. *Quilting Together*. Hancock, N.Y.: Crown Publishers, Inc., 1988. A wonderful guide for traditional Friendship quilts. Many photographs.

Nyhan, Elizabeth F. *Treasury of Patchwork Borders*. New York: Dover Publications, Inc., 1991. A good resource showing many types of borders.

Orlofsky, Myron and Patty Orlofsky. *Quilts in America*. New York: Abbeville Press, 1992. An excellent reference of our quilt heritage as well as history of different types of quilts.

Schlotzhauer, Joyce. *The Curved Two-Patch System*. McLean, Va.: EPM Publications, Inc., 1982.

———. *Curves Unlimited*. McLean, Va.: EPM Publications, Inc., 1986. These two volumes will help you plan and design pieced, curved borders.

Soltow, Willow Ann. *Designing Your Own Quilts*. Radnor, Pa.: Chilton Book Co., 1993. Basic information on quilt composition and design.

Wolfrom, Joen. *The Magical Effects of Color*. Lafayette, Calif.: C & T Publishing, 1992. Use this book as a guide to help increase your confidence about color and design.

About the Authors

Pat Maixner Magaret is a contemporary quiltmaker and teacher whose work is rooted in tradition. She was raised in Nebraska and learned to sew at an early age at her mother's knee. Pat has always enjoyed needle arts and fabric. She graduated from the University of Nebraska with a degree in medical technology and worked in this field until she and her husband, David, started their family. She and David live in Pullman, Washington. All three of their children are away at school.

Donna Ingram Slusser is a professional quiltmaker whose quilts reflect an interest in color and design. Most of her quilts feature machine quilting and back art with whimsical touches. Recently, Donna's quilts have featured her own hand-dyed fabrics and those hand painted by her husband, Lloyd. As a former public school teacher, Donna uses her skills to encourage and inspire her quilting students. Donna lives in a hilltop home near Pullman, Washington. She is inspired by the view, her music, and close ties with nature. An accomplished pipe organist, Donna also enjoys gardening, reading, and caring for a menagerie of pets. Donna and Lloyd have three grown children.

Together, Pat and Donna are two accomplished quiltmakers and teachers who combine traditional styles with contemporary influences in their work. Both are self-taught quilters who began quilting in the early 1980s after retiring from other careers and raising families. They have been team teaching since 1987, and each brings her own unique style and methods to their classes. They are also authors of the best-selling Watercolor Quilts.